Contents

Preface

The greatest problem gardeners have with squash is its frightening productivity even when growing conditions are marginal. When heat and moisture are ideal, its growth is so rapid that the gardener may be picking squash daily.

Summer squash is edible at any size; however there are certain preferences depending upon the type of preparation for which it is intended. There are squash "snobs" who never eat a zucchini or any other summer squash which is more than five inches long. These "babies" are, indeed, delicious and some recipes specify small squash. Medium-sized squash from six to nine inches are adaptable to any kind of preparation, from raw snacks for nibbling to the most sophisticated cream soup or soufflé. The "biggies," which are tougher, seedier, less palatable and less adaptable than younger specimens, are best utilized in bread or other recipes which call for grated squash.

The naive gardener or consumer often equates large size with a healthy, desirable growth rate and economy in production or purchase. While such reasoning may make sense in some circumstances and with some produce, it does not hold true with squash, especially the summer varieties.

Grow lots of squash (it is almost impossible to do otherwise), but remember to pick frequently so that your crop may be cooked at its peak.

Garden Way's
Zucchini Cookbook

by Nancy C. Ralston and Marynor Jordan

This book is dedicated to Carolyn, Deborah, and John.

Printed in the United States   *Ninth Printing, March 1980*

Designed by Linda J. Dawson

Cover by Dawson Design

ISBN: 0-88266-107-8

Becoming Acquainted

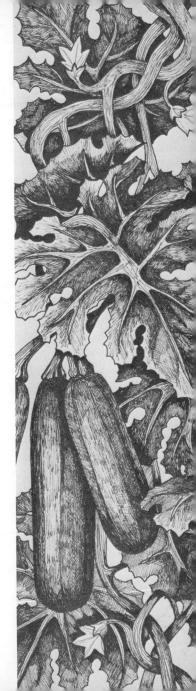

Squash Patch
Squash Schooling
Speaking Nutritionally

Becoming Acquainted

The Squash Patch

Zucchini, one of many "cousins" in the cucurbit family, is joined by many other varieties of summer squash, winter squash, and pumpkins in this book of recipes. Many zucchini recipes are suitable for other summer squash which either may be substituted or used in combination. A rather colorful dish, for instance, can result from combining the dark green zucchini with its golden cousin or a crookneck variety.

Winter squash also are frequently interchangeable in recipes. The squash gardener and cook need not think that all varieties of squash and pumpkin must be available in order to try the full range of squash cookery. One type of summer squash, most likely the zucchini, and one tough-skinned winter squash plus a pumpkin should provide the cook with the basic ingredient to try all the breakfast, lunch, dinner, and snack recipes included in this book.

Squash Schooling

There are two easy ways to learn about squash. One way is to consult comprehensive seed catalogues. New editions of publications generally become available to the eager gardener in January. Thus the colorful, informative pages may be perused in detail before the all-important final order is submitted in early spring. The reader often will find pictures and descriptions of more than 30 squash varieties from which to choose.

The uninitiated easily may become confused by such choices as:

Aristocrat	Goldneck
Blackini	Goldzini
Butterbar	Greyzini
Chefini	Italian Marrow
Cocozelle	Patty Pan
Courgette	Scallops
Crookneck	Straightneck
Cymling	White Bush
Zucchini	

This extensive list refers only to varieties of summer squash.

Confusion is compounded every year as botanists develop additional hybrids with new and fascinating names. Seed catalogues present choices of both bush and vining types of squash. Indeed, there must be a squash for everyone, regardless of space requirements.

Most squash are space-grabbers and may become a nuisance if over-planted. The several bush varieties, although prolific, have less of a tendency to play octopus and overtake other planted areas of your garden.

Many of the recipes in this book can help you deal with the inevitable oversupply, so there is no need for an excessively abundant crop to go to waste.

A later section on canning, freezing, drying, and storing squash explains how simple it is to lay away a supply of summer and winter squash that will last all winter. With a freezer full of yellow and green rounds of crookneck and zucchini, for instance, you can laugh disdainfully at the pathetically bruised and shriveled specimens displayed on supermarket counters for unbelievable prices.

Supermarkets and roadside stands, the second source of "squash schooling," offer colorful collections of winter "cousins" in late summer and early fall. Some varieties, because of differing geographical growing conditions, are available almost all year round. Some of the more widely recognized names include the following:

Acorn	Hubbard
Banana	Hungarian Mammoth
Blue Hubbard	Royal
Buttercup	Spaghetti
Butternut	Sweet Dumplings
Golden Delicious	Sweet Potato
Gold Nugget	Table King
Hercules	Table Queen
Turkish Turban	

The turban squash is sometimes categorized as a gourd. Frequently it is used with other types of gourds in ornamental arrangements. Few people who purchase turbans for this purpose are aware that they are edible.

Most winter squash plants are less compact than summer varieties. Vines extend as much as twenty feet or more. In this sense, the winter squash plant resembles that of the pumpkin more than does its cousin the summer squash. The adjective "winter" may be confusing to some, since these squashes are planted at the same time as "summer" varieties but need a longer growing season. Winter squash is ripe and ready to eat only after the outer shell becomes quite hard. Summer squash, by comparison, has a soft skin which is tender, and edible. Winter squash, because of its hard outer rind, can be stored. It sweetens with age as the starches change to sugar during the storage period. Storage techniques which will guarantee the safekeeping of your prized winter squash crop will be discussed in a later section.

In many recipes winter squash and pumpkin are interchangeable. In fact, a pie made with winter squash is virtually indistinguishable from that made with its pumpkin cousin.

Normally, there are two purposes to be served by the gardener's pumpkin patch. The sugar or sweet pumpkin is counted on to produce the Thanksgiving pie. Younger gardeners in the family are more interested in the traditional jack-o'-lanterns for Halloween, and the bigger the pumpkin, the better! Whatever the primary purpose, the gardener has many varieties from which to choose. In larger gardens the seeds of several types may be sown for comparative purposes. In cases of very limited space, the rather novel midget varieties are recommended.

The following list includes the most common varieties:

Big Max	Funny Face
Big Tom	Jack-O'-Lantern
Cheyenne	Lady Godiva (Naked Seed)
Cinderella	Midget
Cushaw	Sugar

The naked seed pumpkin, Lady Godiva, is sometimes mistakenly categorized as a squash. Its seeds are referred to as "naked" because they have no hard shell and, therefore, need not be cracked before eating. Recipes using these and other seeds are included in a later chapter.

Frequently and erroneously the cushaw pumpkin also is advertised, marketed, grown and/or eaten as a squash. Regardless of what you may call it or how accurate you are in nomenclature, the cushaw makes a delicious pie and, like other edible pumpkins, lends itself beautifully to winter squash recipes.

Speaking Nutritionally

Widespread dietary deficiencies have been discovered at every socio-economic level throughout our country. When it comes to marketing and cooking for our families, we often are not very smart. Home economists are constantly urging us to replace "refined" foods with more natural foodstuffs. "Roughage" has become a household word. In the search for vitamin-packed foods, high in fiber content, the versatile squash stands high on the list.

Summer squash, the dieter's delight, offers a mere five calories per ounce while contributing vitamins A and C, along with iron, calcium, part of the B complex, niacin, riboflavin, and thiamine. Combining summer squash with cheese and/or milk naturally boosts protein and calcium levels.

Not to be outdone, winter squash also is high in nutrient value. A small serving provides enough vitamin A to satisfy the recommended daily requirement. The nutrient bonuses attributed to summer squash also are present. Delicate squash flavors meld tastefully with other vegetables, meat, and dairy products to further increase dietary benefits.

There is a great deal of discussion in medical circles concerning the inclusion of non-digestible fiber in the daily diet. The ability of fibrous material to regulate motility in the gastro-intestinal tract is a proven fact. Since summer squash has a tender, edible skin and seeds containing cellulose, it is an excellent source of unabsorbable roughage.

There is no better way to practice preventive medicine than by indulging in good nutrition. Squash your misconceptions and shop, garden, cook, and eat intelligently for a healthier tomorrow.

Cooking Squash

Cooking Squash

How to Cook Summer Squash

There is no need to pare or remove seeds if the squash is young.

One pound zucchini (three medium about seven inches) equals 3 cups sliced or 2½ cups chopped.

1. Steam whole, cut in half, diced, sliced or cubed.

2. Blanch whole, cut in half, diced, sliced or cubed.

3. Butter-steam sliced, diced, cubed or grated, covered over high heat — watch!

4. Simmer whole, cut in half lengthwise, diced, sliced (rounds or strips), or cubed in boiling salted water.

5. Sauté in margarine or oil diced, sliced, cubed, grated or halved.

6. Halve lengthwise; scoop out pulp and combine with stuffing mixture. Bake for 25-30 minutes at 350°F.

7. Steam, blanch or simmer whole till almost tender. Slice in half lengthwise and scoop out pulp. Combine with cooked ingredients for filling. Bake in a little water for 10 minutes at 375°F.

8. For deep-frying, heat fat 360-375°F. Cut squash into strips or rounds; dredge in flour and fry till golden.

9. For stir-frying, heat oil in wok and stir strips or slices 2-3 minutes.

10. Bake, thinly sliced, in baking dish with other ingredients at 350°F.

How to Cook Winter Squash

The first four methods are useful for filling or stuffing the smaller winter squash such as acorn, butternut, turban, or pattypan.

One pound equals two cups mashed.

1. Cut in half lengthwise; remove seeds and place halves cut side down on baking sheet. Bake in preheated 350°F. oven for 45 minutes. Turn cut side up; loosen squash pulp and add cooked filling (or remove pulp; mash and combine with cooked filling). Return to oven for 15 minutes more.

2. Place cut side up; fill and bake in 350°F. oven for 1 hour.

3. Place whole in baking pan with ¼-inch water. Bake until skin starts to give. Remove from oven and cut in half lengthwise. Remove seeds and stringy portion. Return to pan cut side up. Fill and bake till done.

4. Boil whole and cut in half lengthwise. Remove seeds and stringy portion. Loosen pulp a little; season and stuff. Reheat if necessary.

The following are helpful with the large squashes which are tedious to peel.

5. Boil whole; cut into chunks and peel to eat as is, or mash.

6. Boil large chunks; peel and mash in blender, mixer, or nonelectric food mill.

7. Cut into large chunks. Place skin side up in shallow baking pan. Bake at 375°F.

8. Bake whole at 350-375°F. until skin begins to give. Puncture to let steam escape.

9. Peel; cut into small chunks or slices and sauté or fry.

100,000 Varieties

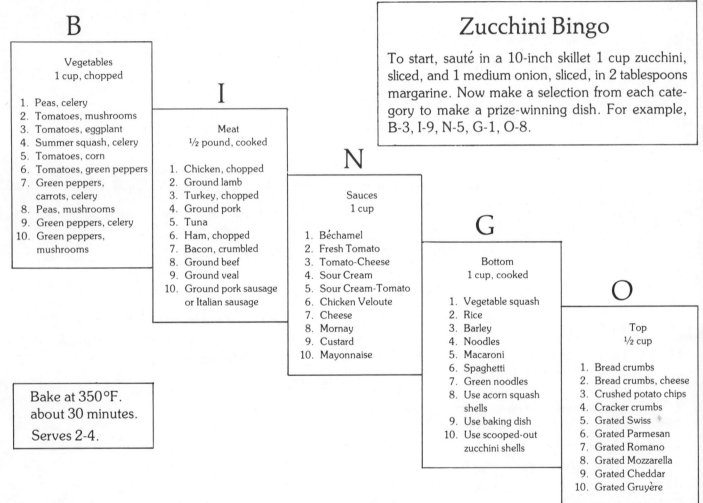

B

Vegetables
1 cup, chopped

1. Peas, celery
2. Tomatoes, mushrooms
3. Tomatoes, eggplant
4. Summer squash, celery
5. Tomatoes, corn
6. Tomatoes, green peppers
7. Green peppers, carrots, celery
8. Peas, mushrooms
9. Green peppers, celery
10. Green peppers, mushrooms

I

Meat
½ pound, cooked

1. Chicken, chopped
2. Ground lamb
3. Turkey, chopped
4. Ground pork
5. Tuna
6. Ham, chopped
7. Bacon, crumbled
8. Ground beef
9. Ground veal
10. Ground pork sausage or Italian sausage

Zucchini Bingo

To start, sauté in a 10-inch skillet 1 cup zucchini, sliced, and 1 medium onion, sliced, in 2 tablespoons margarine. Now make a selection from each category to make a prize-winning dish. For example, B-3, I-9, N-5, G-1, O-8.

N

Sauces
1 cup

1. Béchamel
2. Fresh Tomato
3. Tomato-Cheese
4. Sour Cream
5. Sour Cream-Tomato
6. Chicken Veloute
7. Cheese
8. Mornay
9. Custard
10. Mayonnaise

G

Bottom
1 cup, cooked

1. Vegetable squash
2. Rice
3. Barley
4. Noodles
5. Macaroni
6. Spaghetti
7. Green noodles
8. Use acorn squash shells
9. Use baking dish
10. Use scooped-out zucchini shells

O

Top
½ cup

1. Bread crumbs
2. Bread crumbs, cheese
3. Crushed potato chips
4. Cracker crumbs
5. Grated Swiss
6. Grated Parmesan
7. Grated Romano
8. Grated Mozzarella
9. Grated Cheddar
10. Grated Gruyère

Bake at 350°F.
about 30 minutes.
Serves 2-4.

The Sauce Recipes

1. bechamel
  2 tablespoons margarine
  2 tablespoons flour
  1 cup warm milk

Melt margarine; blend in flour. Stir in milk and simmer until thickened and smooth.

2. fresh tomato
  ½ cup onion, minced
  3 tablespoons olive oil
  2 pounds tomatoes, peeled, seeded and chopped
  1 clove garlic, minced
  1 bay leaf
  1 teaspoon each oregano, parsley, marjoram and sugar

Sauté onion in oil until soft. Add remaining ingredients. Simmer until thickened and reduced.

3. tomato-cheese
  1 cup sharp cheese, shredded
  ½ can tomato soup, undiluted
  1 tablespoon tomato paste
  ½ cup milk

Heat first three ingredients until cheese is melted. Stir in milk.

4. sour cream
  ½ cup sour cream
  1 cup cream soup (chicken, mushroom or shrimp), undiluted
  2 tablespoons dry white wine

Combine all ingredients.

5. sour cream-tomato
  ½ cup sour cream
  ¾ cup tomato purée
  ½ teaspoon paprika

Combine all ingredients.

6. chicken velouté
  2 tablespoons margarine
  2 tablespoons flour
  1 cup chicken broth
  1 egg yolk, beaten with cream (optional)
  Sherry (optional)

Make as for béchamel. Add last two ingredients for a richer sauce.

7. cheese
  2 tablespoons margarine
  1½ tablespoons flour
  1 cup milk
  1 cup sharp cheese, shredded

Make as for béchamel. Stir in cheese until melted.

8. mornay
  2 tablespoons margarine
  2 tablespoons flour
  1 cup cream
  1 egg yolk, slightly beaten
  Parmesan cheese

Make as for béchamel. Stir in egg yolk and cheese.

9. custard
  2 eggs, lightly beaten
  1½ cups milk

Mix together. Pour over ingredients.

10. mayonnaise
  ¾ cup sharp cheese, shredded
  ¼ cup onion, chopped
  1 tablespoon lemon juice
  ½ cup mayonnaise
  Salt
  Chervil

Combine all ingredients.

Seasonings Chart

Zucchini and	Basil	Black Pepper	Cayenne Pepper	Celery Seed	Chives	Cumin	Curry	Dill Seed	Garlic	Ginger	Hot Pepper	Lemon
Beef	X	X	X	X	X	X	X		X	X	X	X
Chicken		X			X		X	X	X	X	X	X
Fish	X	X			X		X	X	X	X		X
Ham												X
Lamb	X	X				X	X	X	X	X		X
Pork	X	X	X						X	X	X	
Sausage		X			X				X		X	
Veal	X	X									X	X
Beets				X				X		X		X
Cabbage		X		X					X			
Carrots		X		X						X		X
Cauliflower	X							X				X
Celery		X			X							X
Corn	X	X	X	X	X					X		
Cucumber	X	X	X	X	X			X				
Eggplant	X	X				X						X
Garbanzos	X	X							X	X		
Green Beans	X	X	X					X	X	X		X
Green Peppers	X	X			X				X		X	X
Onions	X	X	X	X	X		X	X	X			
Mushrooms	X											X
Peas		X	X	X				X				
Spinach	X	X	X									
Tomatoes	X	X			X	X	X		X	X		
Eggs	X	X	X	X	X							
Cheese	X		X	X	X			X			X	
Noodles or Rice	X	X		X	X						X	
Mayonnaise or Sour Cream			X					X				X
Tomato Sauce	X					X			X		X	
White Sauce			X				X					X

The chart lists possible flavorings that you may find helpful in creating your own recipes. Add about one-eighth of a teaspoon of any one or a mixture of the suggested seasonings and correct, if needed, according to your personal preferences. What you like is what is right.

Mint	Mustard Seed	Nutmeg	Onion	Oregano	Paprika	Parsley	Prepared Mustard	Rosemary	Sage	Savory	Sesame Seed	Tarragon	Thyme	White Pepper
X	X	X	X	X	X	X	X	X		X	X	X	X	
		X	X		X	X		X	X		X	X		X
			X		X	X	X					X	X	X
	X	X				X		X						
X	X		X	X	X	X		X			X		X	
	X	X		X	X	X		X	X	X	X	X	X	
	X	X	X		X	X	X		X	X			X	
	X			X			X	X				X	X	X
X		X						X						
			X	X	X									X
X		X				X					X		X	
		X		X	X			X		X	X	X		X
X	X				X					X	X		X	X
	X		X	X		X					X			
X	X		X		X			X						
				X		X		X					X	
			X	X		X		X						
X		X	X				X				X	X	X	
	X		X	X							X	X	X	
	X	X	X		X									X
	X		X	X	X							X		
X		X	X							X	X			
		X	X	X			X				X			X
		X	X	X		X						X		X
		X				X		X			X	X		X
		X		X		X	X	X		X			X	X
		X		X		X								
X			X			X						X		X
			X	X		X								
X		X				X					X	X		X

Appetizers & Snacks

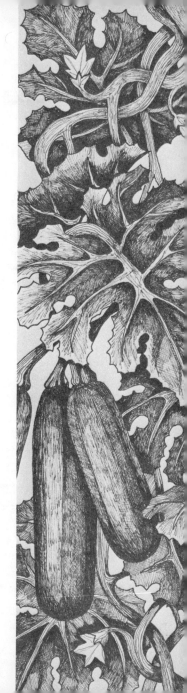

Antipasto
Hors d'Oeuvres
Canapes
Sandwiches
Seed Snacks
Snack Chips

Appetizers & Snacks

Antipasto

The Italians have a habit of serving delicious and imaginative tidbits as appetizers or an antipasto, meaning "before food." The only problem with this custom is that all of the components of the antipasto are so good and so filling that you can get carried away with trying a dab of everything and forget that dinner is yet to come!

Ordinarily, antipasto consists of several cold meats, selections of cheese, and vegetables, marinated or raw, of all descriptions.

The zucchini, in various marinades, makes a very appropriate antipasto contribution.

zucchini and cauliflower à la Greque

Slice zucchini, break cauliflower into florets, julienne (cut into long, thin strips) the green pepper. Combine all other ingredients in saucepan. Bring to boil, add vegetables. Reduce heat and simmer until tender but not mushy. Place in large bowl or crock, cover and refrigerate. Serve cold. *Note:* Other ingredients may be combined with the zucchini: green beans, Brussels sprouts, carrots, eggplant, onions, mushrooms, artichoke hearts, cherry tomatoes, small whole beets, red kidney beans, garbanzos, etc.

5-6 small zucchini
1 head cauliflower
1 green pepper
½ cup olive oil
1 cup lemon juice
2 lemon slices
1 teaspoon salt
1 clove garlic, crushed
½ teaspoon coarsely ground pepper
1 teaspoon thyme
¼ teaspoon hot pepper sauce

dilled zucchini

2 medium summer squash
salt
Olive oil or margarine,
   melted
Dill seed

Cut squash lengthwise enough times to make sticks. Cover with boiling water to which salt has been added and cook for 5-6 minutes until tender. Drain well. Drizzle with oil or melted margarine. Sprinkle with dill seed or fresh dill weed.

zucchini vinaigrette

¼ cup dry sherry or ver-
   mouth
1 envelope Italian dressing
   mix
½ cup olive oil
¼ cup white vinegar
3 tablespoons chives,
   chopped
3 tablespoons sweet pickles,
   chopped
2 tablespoons parsley,
   chopped
3 tablespoons green pepper,
   chopped
4 medium-small zucchini,
   golden zucchini or other
   summer squash

Combine wine, dressing mix, and all other seasonings and mix thoroughly. Slice squash lengthwise in sticks of appropriate size. Place in pan of water, bring to boil and simmer about 4 minutes until tender crisp. Drain well; pat dry with paper towel. Arrange zucchini sticks in shallow dish. Pour marinade over them. Cover and chill overnight. Spoon dressing over zucchini occasionally. Serve cold.

Hors d'Oeuvres

The French, with their hors d'oeuvres meaning "outside of the essential part of the meal," are very imaginative in preparing appetizers. Strips or rounds of summer squash served with tasty dips make delicious and nutritious hors d'oeuvres. Such appetizers as raw squash, served singly or in combination with other raw vegetables, provide you and your guests with the beginnings of a wholesome diet. How much more nutritious and less caloric than the grease-laden potato chip.

simple curry dip

1 cup plain yogurt
1 tablespoon curry powder

Mix well and serve.

cottage cheese dip

1 carton (12 ounces) cream-style cottage cheese
1 tablespoon fresh chives, chopped
½ teaspoon hot pepper sauce

Blend well and serve. Makes 1½ cups.

zucchini sticks

Cut young, tender squash into strips of appropriate size for dunking. Serve with seasoned salt and/or one or more of the following cocktail dips:

blue cheese dip

1 3-ounce package cream cheese
1 ounce crumbled blue cheese or Roquefort
2 teaspoons chili sauce
½ teaspoon paprika
½ teaspoon Worcestershire sauce
¼ teaspoon salt
Pinch of white pepper

Blend well and serve. Makes 1 cup.

1 zucchini or other summer
  squash
1 3-ounce package
  cream cheese
1 tablespoon chopped green
  onions, tops included
2 teaspoons parsley,
  chopped
1 teaspoon sour cream
½ teaspoon white vinegar

zucchini rounds

Peel squash with potato peeler. Use end of peeler to core the squash, removing seed section. Combine all other ingredients and stuff squash with this mixture. Slice and serve chilled.

Canapés

A canapé, another French standby, is a snack or appetizer consisting of delectable tidbits spread or layered upon a small piece of toast or bread. Canapés are usually more substantial, a bit fancier, and somewhat more formal than the typical hors d'oeuvre. A tray full of elaborately prepared canapés is, indeed, a sight to see.

Substituting zucchini slices for toast or bread rounds is another example of how to cut calories and yet serve tasty and decorative appetizers.

zucchini canapés

Small zucchini or other summer squash may be sliced in rounds ¼-inch thick. Salt, then drain on paper toweling. Top with any of the following and serve as snacks.

Tuna fish salad
Ham salad
Hardboiled egg slices,
topped with a rolled
anchovy

Cheese ribbons or rosettes
(processed cheese spread
in pressurized containers)
Cream cheese and minced
clams

Sandwiches

Carrying the canapé idea a bit further, more substantial offerings in the form of bona fide sandwiches are also possible, using larged sized slices of summer squash. The variety of possible sandwich fillings is limited only by one's imagination and taste preferences. Here are some possibilities.

zucchiniwiches

Slice zucchini (about 2½-3-inches in diameter) into ¼-inch rounds. Spread one slice with a mixture such as one of the these suggestions. Top with another slice. Sprinkle with paprika. Serve with soup or as an appetizer.

Tuna, ham, or chicken salad
Pimiento, smoky, or Roquefort-cream cheese
Deviled egg salad

2 cups zucchini, grated and drained
1 cup carrots, grated
¼ cup celery, chopped
⅓ cup peanut butter
⅓ cup mayonnaise
8 slices cracked wheat bread
Lettuce leaves

zucchini-peanut butter sandwich

Combine squash with carrot, celery, and mayonnaise. Spread peanut butter on four bread slices. Top with vegetable mixture and lettuce leaf. Complete sandwich by adding bread slice spread with additional mayonnaise, if desired.

1 medium zucchini or other
summer squash
8 slices pumpernickel or dark
rye bread
1 4½-ounce can deviled
ham
1 teaspoon horseradish
4 tablespoons mayonnaise,
yogurt or cottage cheese
Seasoned salt

squash sandwich

Slice squash as thinly as possible. Mix deviled ham and horse-radish and spread on four slices of bread. Mix other ingredients and spread on remaining pieces of bread. Layer on squash slices and top with ham-horseradish bread slices. Cut sandwiches and serve.

Seed Snacks

A novelty member of the cucurbit family is the naked-seed squash or Lady Godiva. One gardening catalog advertises the seeds in terms of "Grow your own snacks." This rather unusual pumpkin-shaped fruit with green markings produces shell-less seeds which may be eaten either raw or toasted. Since they are "naked," these nutritious, protein-rich seeds need no tedious hulling.

Lady Godiva Naked Seeds. To obtain home-grown squash seed snacks, simply cut a Lady Godiva in half and scoop out the naked seeds. Rinse seeds, separating them from squash fibers, and place them on absorbent paper or cloth towels to dry for several days.

If you prefer toasted seeds, place them on an oiled cookie sheet in a 350°F oven and toast until brown and crunchy, or heat seeds in a skillet on top of the stove or over a campfire. In either case, the seeds should be lightly lubricated with cooking oil. The seeds should be stirred frequently and if the skillet method is chosen, a lid is essential since the seeds have a tendency to "pop" much like popcorn.

Season browned seeds with salt and pepper and serve as a tasty snack or hors d'oeuvre.

Other cucurbit seeds which are not "naked" are also edible. An additional step is all that is necessary to prepare them for nibbling. After toasting, other squash and pumpkin seeds, like sunflower seeds, must be cracked so that the shells may be removed.

Food Value of Seeds. Plant protein is found in greatest concentration in seeds. Analogous to the egg of the animal world, a well-known source of protein, squash and pumpkin seeds are also store-houses of nutritious food elements.

toasted seed snacks

Seeds from squash or pumpkin first should be separated from fibers. Then cover seeds with boiling water to which salt has been added. Reduce heat and simmer gently for 1½-2 hours. Spread seeds on a cookie sheet. Using a pastry brush, coat with safflower or peanut oil. Salt generously. Bake in a slow 250°F. oven until adequately browned.

Pumpkin seeds
Sunflower seeds
Sesame seeds
Wheat germ, toasted
Pumpkin seed butter (see under "Breads and Butter")
Peanut butter

pumpkin seed balls

Prepare seeds as for baked or toasted. Mix with remaining ingredients. Add salt, if needed. Shape into tiny balls.

curried toasted seeds

Heat mixture of oil and seasonings. Stir in seeds. Line a cookie sheet with aluminum foil. Spread seeds on sheet and bake at 350°F. until crisp.

¼ cup peanut or safflower oil
2 teaspoons curry powder
1 teaspoon Worcestershire sauce
2 drops hot pepper sauce
Pumpkin or squash seeds

baked seed snacks

Separate squash or pumpkin seeds from fibrous material. Soak overnight in mixture of 2 teaspoons salt per 1 cup water. Set oven at 300°F. Bake 30-45 minutes. Do not allow to brown.

Snack Chips

Winter squash and pumpkin, not to be entirely outdone by their summer cousins in the snack category, lend themselves to a recipe for a hot appetizer or snack. Some people prefer a sweeter taste, in which case sugar may be substituted for the garlic salt.

½ pound raw winter squash
    or pumpkin
½ teaspoon garlic
1½ tablespoons curry powder
    Oil for cooking

squash/pumpkin snack chips

Peel and seed squash/pumpkin. Slice as thin as possible into potato chip size. Place in refrigerator to chill for 45 minutes in a bowl of ice water. Drain well. Dry with paper towels. Deep fry until browned. Sprinkle with combined seasonings.

Breads & Butter

Breads & Butter

Accustomed as we are to uninspiring commercially processed bread, we are likely to have become complacent about tasteless and virtually nutritionless bread.

Breadmaking is, admittedly, a time-consuming activity and many cooks are not interested enough to undertake such a project. Others have made noble breadmaking attempts only to fail because of inadequate recipes, poor equipment, yeast failure, or inadvertent mistakes. How demoralizing to acquire all the proper ingredients, combine them, knead the dough interminably, impatiently survive the risings, bake the bread, and yet at serving time, discover the whole aromatic mess won't even yield to a carving knife!

Have no fear. The squash bread recipes included here are virtually foolproof, and the results are so delicious you will receive all sorts of accolades. Serve any one of these great breads with one of your favorite squash soups or stews and you will please everyone who sits at your table — and sneak in extra nutrition, too.

zucchini bread

Mix first 6 ingredients. Sift together dry ingredients; combine with zucchini mixture. Add raisins and/or nuts. Makes 2 loaves. Bake at 350°F for 1 hour; cool 10 minutes. Remove from pan. Individual loaves make welcome gifts. You may substitute ½ cup coarse bran for ½ cup of the flour.

3 eggs, lightly beaten
1 cup salad oil
1 cup sugar
2 cups zucchini, grated and drained
2 teaspoons vanilla
3¼ cups flour
1 teaspoon baking powder
1 teaspoon baking soda
3 teaspoons cinnamon
1 teaspoon salt
¾ cup raisins
1 cup nuts, chopped

3 eggs
1 cup salad oil
1½ cups brown sugar, packed
1 cup zucchini, grated and
    drained
1 cup carrots, grated
2 teaspoons vanilla
2½ cups all-purpose flour
½ cup bran cereal
1 teaspoon baking soda
1 teaspoon baking powder
1 teaspoon salt
3 teaspoons cinnamon
1 cup chopped nuts

zucchini-carrot bread

Preheat oven to 350°F. Have ready 2 well-greased 8½ × 4½-inch loaf pans. In large mixing bowl, beat eggs with oil. Stir in sugar, zucchini, carrot, and vanilla. Sift in flour, baking soda, baking powder, salt, and cinnamon, and blend remaining ingredients into zucchini mixture, adding nuts last. Bake 1-1½ hours at 350°F.

2 eggs
¼ cup milk
1 cup cooked squash,
    mashed
⅔ cup cooking oil
1 cup brown sugar
½ cup sorghum or honey
2 cups all-purpose flour
1 teaspoon baking soda
½ teaspoon baking powder
½ teaspoon salt
½ teaspoon nutmeg
½ teaspoon cinnamon

winter squash bread

Combine first 6 ingredients and mix well. Sift in remaining ingredients; beat at medium speed 2 minutes. Turn into greased 9 × 5-inch loaf pan. Bake in 350°F. oven about 65 minutes. Raisins and nuts may be added.

pumpkin nut bread

Beat oil, sugar, and eggs at high speed 3 minutes. Sift together dry ingredients, add, and stir in remaining ingredients. Beat until batter is smooth. Pour into greased 9 × 5-inch loaf pan. Bake at 350°F. for 1 hour.

1/3 cup cooking oil
1 1/3 cups sugar
   2 eggs
   1 cup cooked pumpkin, mashed
1/4 cup milk
1 2/3 cups flour
   1 teaspoon baking soda
1/2 teaspoon baking powder
1/2 teaspoon salt
1/2 teaspoon pumpkin pie spice
1/2 teaspoon cinnamon
1/2 cup nuts

whole wheat squash rolls

1 package yeast
3 cups whole wheat flour
2 teaspoons salt
1/4 cup sugar
3 tablespoons cooking oil
3/4 cup water or milk
1/2 cup winter squash, mashed
3 tablespoons molasses

Combine dry ingredients in large mixing bowl. Heat oil and liquid in a saucepan to 120°F. (lukewarm). Add squash and molasses. Cool to lukewarm; stir into dry ingredients making a stiff dough. Add more flour if necessary. Knead 10 minutes on a lightly floured board. Place in a greased bowl. Turn to greased surface and cover with a towel. Let rise in a warm place until double or about an hour. Roll to 1/2-inch thickness and cut into 2-inch rounds or shape into balls. Brush tops with oil. Place 1 inch apart on a greased baking sheet. Cover and let rise about 45 minutes. Bake in a preheated 425°F. oven for 20 minutes.

Makes about one dozen.

2 cups sugar
1/3 cup molasses
1 cup cooked pumpkin,
   mashed
1 cup applesauce
2/3 cup oil
3 eggs
1/3 cup milk
3 2/3 cups flour
1 1/2 teaspoons baking powder
2 teaspoons baking soda
2 teaspoons cinnamon
1 teaspoon nutmeg
1 teaspoon vanilla
1 cup chopped nuts
1 cup raisins or dates

pumpkin-applesauce tea bread

At medium speed beat together first 7 ingredients. Sift in dry ingredients, then add remaining ingredients and mix well. Pour into 2 well-greased 9 × 5-inch loaf pans. Bake at 350°F. for 1 hour. Cool 10 minutes in pans. Wrap in foil and store overnight.

zucchini pan rolls

Stir together first 4 ingredients. Combine with warm liquid and add all at once to remaining ingredients in a large bowl. Knead dough about 10 minutes to make a soft firm dough. Grease surface of dough and let rise in a warm place until doubled. Turn out on floured board and knead lightly. Shape into rolls and let rise again about 30 minutes. Preheat oven to 400°F. Place rolls in pan on middle rack and immediately lower heat to 375°F. Bake 15-20 minutes. Tops may be sprayed with salt water and sprinkled with poppy or sesame seeds.

1 teaspoon flour
2 teaspoons honey
1/2 cup warm water
1 package yeast
1 cup warm water or milk
2 tablespoons oil
3 1/2 cups flour
1/2 teaspoon salt
2/3 cup zucchini, grated and
   drained

zucchini stuffing

In a saucepan, cook celery and onion in margarine until tender. Remove from heat. Add remaining ingredients and mix well.
Makes enough for a 10-pound bird.

½ cup celery, chopped
½ cup onion, chopped
3 tablespoons margarine
4 cups bread cubes
4 cups zucchini, chopped
2 eggs slightly beaten
½ cup shredded cheese
1 teaspoon salt
1 teaspoon poultry seasoning

1 egg, beaten
½ cup cooked pumpkin
⅓ cup milk
¼ cup margarine, melted
1 teaspoon cinnamon
¼ teaspoon salt
2 tablespoons sugar
1 teaspoon baking powder
1 cup all-purpose flour

pumpkin muffins

Beat together first 4 ingredients. Stir briefly into sifted dry ingredients. Batter will still be lumpy. Fill well-greased muffin tins ⅔ full. Bake at 400°F. for 25 minutes.

pumpkin seed butter

Combine all ingredients in electric blender and blend until preferred texture is achieved. *Note:* This is delicious on any type of bread. Try it with pumpkin muffins.

½ cup raw "naked" Lady Godiva seeds
½ cup peanuts
¼ cup sesame seeds
2 tablespoons cooking oil
½ cup honey
Salt

Casseroles

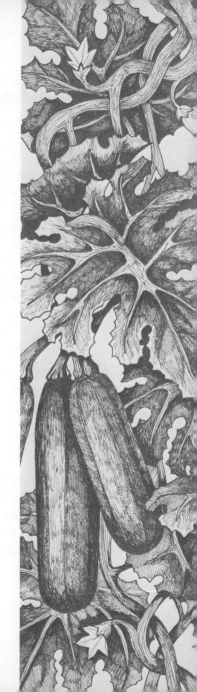

Casseroles

Squashes with Meat

Actually, a casserole is the container in which a meal is cooked and frequently served rather than the recipe or concoction itself. Many of us, under harried conditions, have expressed gratitude to whatever genius invented the casserole. That "genius" was the first prehistoric human who devised a vessel in which to cook whatever was available. The modern-day cook, appreciative of the time- and effort-saving practice of preparing an entire meal in a single pot, has many utensils from which to choose, ranging from the old faithful cast-iron Dutch oven to the automatic slow cooker so popular today.

Members of the versatile squash family combined with other vegetables, cheeses, meats, herbs, and spices can produce many tasty one-dish meals.

zucchini stroganoff

Place ground beef and onion in a 10-inch skillet. Cook until beef loses pink color. Spread over beef mixture the mushroom soup, noodles, zucchini, and seasonings. Simmer covered until the noodles are done. Stir in sour cream and warm through. *Note:* Try other ground meats such as pork sausage (marjoram or savory), lamb (basil or oregano), or veal (rosemary or tarragon).

Serves 2.

½ pound ground beef
¼ cup onion, chopped
½ can mushroom soup
1 cup egg noodles
1 cup sliced zucchini
Seasoned salt and pepper
½ teaspoon chervil or basil
⅔ cup sour cream

1/3 cup olive oil
2 cloves garlic, minced
1 cup onion, chopped
3 medium zucchini, sliced
3 green or red sweet peppers, cut in strips
1 medium eggplant, thinly sliced
1 tablespoon oregano
3 tablespoons flour
Salt and pepper
2 cups tomatoes, peeled, seeded, and chopped
Leftover meat loaf slices
3 slices Mozzarella cheese

zucchini-meat loaf ratatouille

In a large heavy skillet, heat oil; add garlic and onion. Sauté until onion is transparent. In a large bowl toss zucchini, peppers, eggplant, oregano, flour, salt, and pepper until well-combined. Add this mixture to the skillet, topping with the tomatoes. Cover and cook over low heat 1 hour. Uncover and continue cooking until very thick. In a 1½-quart casserole start with a layer of the zucchini mixture then add meat loaf and continue until casserole is filled. Top with Mozzarella cheese. Heat thoroughly in 350° F. oven. *Note:* This dish is good hot or cold and makes an excellent omelet filling with or without the meat loaf.

Serves 4.

zucchini-lamb shank provençale

Insert garlic slivers into lamb shanks. Brown meat in cooking oil. Add onions and cook until soft. Pour off excess fat. Add tomatoes, seasonings, and liquid. Bake uncovered at 350°F. in Dutch oven for 1½ hours. Add zucchini and mix well. Add more water if necessary and continue to bake 30 minutes more.

Serves 6.

6 lamb shanks
2 cloves garlic, slivered
2 tablespoons cooking oil
3 medium onions, diced
2 cups tomatoes, peeled and drained
3 teaspoons salt
1 bay leaf
½ cup water or dry red wine
3 medium zucchini, sliced

zucchini and tuna

3 tablespoons margarine
1 cup shredded zucchini, drained
1/2 cup green pepper, chopped
1/2 cup celery, sliced
1/3 cup onion, chopped
1 can tuna, drained
2 tablespoons flour
1 cup milk
2 tablespoons parsley
1/2 cup grated Cheddar cheese
1 teaspoon salt
1/2 teaspoon dill
6 ounces noodles, cooked
   Cracker crumbs

In large saucepan melt margarine. Stir in zucchini, green peppers, celery, and onion; cook until soft. Blend in next 7 ingredients until thickened. Add cooked noodles. Place in 1-quart casserole. Sprinkle with crumbs. Warm at 325°F. until heated through.

Serves 2-3.

1½ pounds chicken pieces or
1 pound cooked chicken meat
3/4 cup seasoned flour
1/2 cup margarine
1/4 cup cooking oil
2 cups zucchini, 1/2-inch slices
1 tablespoon lemon juice
1 tablespoon Hungarian paprika
4 ounces noodles
1/2 cup sour cream

zucchini-chicken hungarian

Coat chicken pieces with seasoned flour. Melt 1/4 cup margarine and the cooking oil in a large skillet. Sauté chicken until tender. (If using cooked chicken meat, place in baking dish to warm in a low oven.) In a saucepan, melt the remaining margarine and cook in it the zucchini, lemon juice, and paprika 8-10 minutes. Cook noodles; drain and combine with zucchini. Blend in half the sour cream. Place in greased, 1½-quart casserole with chicken. Top with remaining sour cream.

Serves 2-3.

1 cup dry bread crumbs
  Cold roast lamb, sliced or
  cubed (about ½ pound)
3 medium zucchini, sliced
2 medium tomatoes, peeled
  and sliced
1 teaspoon rosemary
  Salt and pepper
  Margarine

zucchini-leftover lamb scallop

Layer bread crumbs in bottom of baking pan or 1-quart greased casserole. Alternate layers of meat, squash, and tomatoes. Sprinkle meat layers with crushed rosemary leaves. Season vegetable layers with salt, pepper, and pats of margarine. Heat oven to 350°F. Bake for 45 minutes.

Serves 2.

the pumpkin is the casserole

Remove lid of pumpkin and retain. Scoop out seeds and stringy portion. Score inside several times and rub interior with salt and pepper. Place pumpkin upside down in large shallow pan with ¼-inch water. Place lid in pan beside pumpkin. Bake at 350°F. for one hour or until tender. Drain. In a skillet, sauté onion, green pepper, and garlic in margarine. Add ground beef and seasonings and simmer until meat is lightly browned. Cook with tomatoes, broth, and wine until liquid is reduced considerably. Stir in cooked rice and mix thoroughly. Stuff pumpkin with this mixture. Top with grated cheese and return to oven until cheese is melted. Replace lid until serving time. Serve from the pumpkin. The pumpkin pulp may be scooped out and served also.

Serves 6.

1 5-6 pound pumpkin
  Salt and pepper
1 medium onion, minced
1 green pepper, minced
1 clove garlic, minced
¼ cup margarine
1 pound ground beef
½ teaspoon thyme
½ teaspoon salt
¼ teaspoon pepper
3 tomatoes, peeled and
  quartered
1 cup beef broth or bouillon
2 tablespoons dry white wine
1½ cups cooked rice
½ cup Cheddar cheese,
  grated

zucchini with bacon

Cook zucchini in small amount of boiling salted water about 5 minutes. Mix together next 3 ingredients and fold in egg white. Layer in 1-quart casserole half the squash, egg mixture, and bacon. Repeat. Top with bread crumbs. Bake in preheated 350°F oven for 20 minutes.

Serves 2-3.

2½ cups zucchini, thinly sliced
½ cup sour cream
1 egg yolk, slightly beaten
1 tablespoon flour
1 egg white, stiffly beaten
1 cup Cheddar cheese, shredded
3 slices bacon, crumbled
⅓ cup bread crumbs, tossed with
1 tablespoon melted margarine

¼ pound bulk pork sausage
2 tablespoons onion, chopped
⅓ cup crushed oyster crackers or saltines
⅓ cup Parmesan cheese
¾ cup milk
2 eggs, slightly beaten
2 cups zucchini, cooked, drained, and chopped
1 teaspoon salt
Dash thyme
Parslied-garlic salt
Buttered crumbs

zucchini-pork sausage scallop

In skillet cook sausage and onion until sausage is brown; drain. Remove from heat. Combine all ingredients and place in 1-quart greased casserole. Sprinkle on buttered crumbs. Bake in 350°F. oven till set. *Note:* To make a meatless version, omit sausage and thyme; layer zucchini with onion, crackers, cheese, and seasonings. Mix the 2 eggs with 1 cup milk and pour over until just barely covers. Top with crumbs. Bake at 350°F. about 30 minutes.

Serves 2.

zucchini and italian sausage

Cook zucchini in small amount of boiling salted water about 5 minutes; chop. Brown sausage and drain off excess fat. Combine bread crumbs, Parmesan, zucchini, sausage, parsley, seasoning, and egg yolks. Fold in egg whites. Add vegetables gently. Place in 1-quart greased casserole. Sprinkle with reserved crumbs. Bake in preheated 325°F oven for 45 minutes.

Serves 2.

1 pound zucchini, sliced thinly (3 cups)
4 ounces bulk Italian sausage
1/3 cup bread crumbs, 1 tablespoon reserved
1/3 cup grated Parmesan
Salt and pepper
1 tablespoon parsley
2 egg yolks, slightly beaten
2 egg whites, stiffly beaten
1/4 cup green pepper, chopped
1/4 cup onion, chopped
1/3 cup mushroom pieces

1 pound ground veal
1 1/2 cups tomato sauce
1/4 cup red wine
4 medium zucchini, thinly sliced
1 teaspoon oregano
1/2 teaspoon basil
1 teaspoon garlic salt
1 3/4 cups Mozzarella, shredded
1/4 cup Parmesan cheese
1/4 cup seasoned bread crumbs

zucchini-ground veal italian

Brown veal in a skillet. Combine tomato sauce, wine, zucchini, oregano, basil, and garlic salt. Simmer about 10 minutes. Add to veal. Layer veal mixture and Mozzarella in a 1 1/2-quart casserole. Sprinkle with Parmesan and bread crumbs. Heat in a 350°F. oven until cheese is melted. *Note:* A bottom layer of spaghetti squash would add interest and volume.

Serves 4.

zucchini-veal cutlet españa

Dip cutlets into beaten egg and dredge in crumbs. In a 10-inch skillet, brown lightly in olive oil. Layer meat with tomatoes and seasoning. Cover mixture and simmer 30 minutes. Cut zucchini into ¼-inch slices and place over veal-tomato mixture. Simmer 25-30 minutes.

Serves 6.

6 veal cutlets
1 egg, beaten
¾ cup dry bread crumbs
¼ cup olive oil
2 cups tomatoes, peeled
  and sliced
1½ teaspoons salt
⅓ teaspoon oregano
  Salt and pepper
  Parmesan cheese
3 medium zucchini

1 pound bulk pork sausage
1 teaspoon onion, minced
2 medium squash, sliced
½ cup dry bread crumbs
½ cup milk
½ cup American cheese,
  grated
½ cup mixed vegetables,
  cooked
¼ teaspoon oregano
¼ teaspoon parsley flakes
¼ teaspoon savory
¼ teaspoon celery or mustard
  seed
2 eggs, beaten

zucchini-sausage combo

Crumble sausage; add onion and cook slowly until pork is lightly browned. Remove excess fat. Simmer squash in salted water until barely tender. Drain and add to meat along with bread crumbs, milk, cheese, vegetables, and seasonings. Stir eggs in slowly. Pour into 1½-quart greased casserole. Bake 30 minutes at 325°F.

Serves 4.

zucchini-barbecued chicken

Place zucchini in bottom of shallow 1½-quart greased baking pan. Arrange chicken over zucchini. Combine remaining ingredients and pour over chicken. Bake, covered, at 375°F. for 1 hour, basting every 15 minutes with the liquid.

Serves 2-3.

2 medium zucchini, ¼-inch slices
2 chicken breasts, boned
  Salt and pepper
⅔ cup barbecue sauce
½ teaspoon oregano
½ teaspoon basil
¼ cup onion, chopped
2 teaspoons sherry

2 pounds lamb cut into
  1-inch cubes
1 cup onions, diced
1 tablespoon olive oil
2 tablespoons margarine
2 teaspoons tomato paste
1 teaspoon thyme
  Salt and pepper
1 cup water (or stock)
3 cups zucchini, diced
1 cup yellow summer
  squash, diced
1½ cups carrots, diced
1 cup onions, diced
1 can garbanzo beans,
  drained
  Rice

zucchini-lamb pilaf

Brown meat and sauté onion in oil and margarine. Add tomato paste, seasonings, water or stock, and vegetables. Simmer 30-40 minutes until meat and vegetables are tender. Serve over hot buttered rice.

Serves 6.

zucchini-shrimp supreme

Sauté zucchini, onion, and green pepper in 4 tablespoons margarine until tender. Combine with sour cream, shrimp soup, and 1½ cups bread crumbs. Turn into 1½-quart greased casserole. Top with remaining crumbs and margarine. Bake in 350° F. oven for 30 minutes.

Serves 6.

6 cups zucchini, sliced
  ½-inch thick or
2 cups cooked winter
  squash, mashed
½ cup onion, chopped
½ cup green pepper,
  chopped
6 tablespoons margarine,
  melted
1 cup sour cream
1 can condensed cream of
  shrimp soup
2 cups seasoned bread
  crumbs
¼ cup Parmesan cheese

5 cups butternut squash,
  baked
½ cup onions, chopped
½ pound ground lamb
¼ cup tomato sauce
¼ teaspoon nutmeg
2 tablespoons margarine
2 tablespoons flour
1 cup milk
½ cup Mozzarella, grated
  Bread crumbs

butternut-lamb deluxe

Scoop out flesh from butternut. Cook onions and lamb in skillet until pink color is gone. Add tomato sauce and nutmeg. In large saucepan melt margarine; add flour and stir in milk and cheese until thickened. Add lamb mixture and squash. Sprinkle bread crumbs on bottom of shallow, greased 1-quart baking dish. Spread squash mixture evenly and top with more crumbs. Bake at 325°F. about 20 minutes. *Note:* For extra consistency and richness, stir into cooked squash ⅓ cup more bread crumbs.

Serves 4.

1 butternut squash (2 pounds)
2 tablespoons margarine
¾ cup onion, minced
2 cups toasted croutons
½ teaspoon poultry seasoning
½ teaspoon salt
Pepper
1 cup chicken broth
2 cups cooked turkey or chicken, diced
½ cup Cheddar cheese, shredded

butternut-turkey casserole

Cut squash in half lengthwise and discard seeds. Bake, cut side down in baking pan at 350°F. for 50-60 minutes until squash is tender. Scoop out pulp and mash. Sauté onions in margarine; add toasted croutons and seasonings. Add broth, mashed squash, and diced turkey. Place mixture in a 1½-quart greased casserole. Bake at 350°F for 20 minutes. Sprinkle cheese on top and return to oven until cheese is melted.

Serves 6.

zucchini-coq au vin

Slice squash ¼-inch thick. Pour ½ of the olive oil into a large skillet or Dutch oven. Sauté minced garlic and squash 8-10 minutes. Remove from pan. Add additional olive oil and chicken pieces. Brown pieces thoroughly. Season with salt and pepper. Layer zucchini and tomato slices over chicken, adding wine and other seasonings. Continue cooking over low heat 25-30 minutes until chicken is tender. Transfer chicken and vegetables to serving platter. Add stock to pot and simmer, stirring frequently until sauce is smooth and somewhat reduced. Pour over zucchini and chicken. This may be served over rice, spaghetti, or noodles.

Serves 4.

2 pounds zucchini, sliced
4 tablespoons olive oil
4 cloves garlic, minced
4 chicken legs and thighs
Salt and pepper
1 medium tomato, peeled and sliced
2 cups dry white wine or vermouth
¼ teaspoon basil
¼ teaspoon rosemary
¼ teaspoon tarragon
½ cup chicken stock or bouillon

zucchini-ground beef italian

In olive oil sauté onions, green peppers, and garlic 2 minutes. Stir in ground beef; cook until browned. Stir in remaining ingredients. Turn into 1-quart casserole. Bake 30 minutes at 350°F.

Serves 2.

1 tablespoon olive oil
½ cup onions, chopped
1 med. green pepper, chopped
1 clove garlic, minced
½ pound ground beef
1 cup zucchini, thinly sliced
1 cup ripe tomatoes, peeled, seeded, and chopped
½ teaspoon oregano
½ teaspoon basil
Dash of hot-pepper sauce
Salt and pepper

1 pound zucchini, thinly sliced
2½ tablespoons flour
2 tablespoons margarine, melted
1 cup milk
½ cup Cheddar cheese, shredded
1-2 cups cooked ham, chopped
1 medium onion, sliced
Salt and pepper
1 cup bread crumbs, mixed with
3 tablespoons melted margarine
¼ cup Parmesan cheese

zucchini-ham delight

Cook zucchini in boiling salted water about 5 minutes; drain. Add flour to margarine and stir in milk and cheese. Cook until thickened and add ham. Place zucchini in bottom of shallow 1½-quart greased baking dish. Arrange onion rings over zucchini. Salt and pepper. Spoon sauce over vegetables. Mix crumbs with Parmesan and sprinkle over top. Bake in preheated 350°F. oven about 20 minutes.

Serves 4.

Egg Dishes

Soufflés
Crêpes
Omelets
Quiches
Waffles
Pancakes
Custards

Egg Dishes

Soufflés

The French verb *souffler* means "to blow," and the thought of attempting a soufflé is enough to blow the mind of some cooks. This is unfortunate, for a delicious soufflé is not that difficult to prepare. Granted, there are some pitfalls to avoid, but this is true with many dishes.

A good recipe, steady heat and a well-prepared soufflé dish are the only requirements. The soufflé dish should be well-buttered and floured and of an appropriate size. The height of a soufflé dish may be extended by encircling it with a strip of wax paper. A long double thickness of the paper tied around the dish so that it extends 2 inches above the rim will give your soufflé the chance to puff up or "blow up" beautifully without fear of its overflowing the limits of the container.

Pumpkin and winter squash are interchangeable in these recipes.

pumpkin-ginger soufflé

Mash pumpkin pulp. Combine in saucepan with maple syrup, nutmeg, ginger, salt, and margarine. Cook and stir over low heat 5 minutes. Beat egg yolks and add to pumpkin mixture. Heat thoroughly. Fold stiffly beaten egg whites along with brown sugar into pumpkin mixture. Pour into prepared 4-cup soufflé dish. Preheat oven to 350°F. Bake for 30 minutes.

Serves 4.

1 cup cooked pumpkin pulp
¼ cup maple syrup
¼ teaspoon nutmeg
¼ teaspoon ginger
⅛ teaspoon salt
2 tablespoons margarine
6 eggs, separated
3 tablespoons brown sugar

4 medium zucchini, peeled
  and cubed
1 tablespoon lemon juice
2 teaspoons salt
2 tablespoons margarine
2 tablespoons flour
1 cup chicken broth or milk
4 eggs, separated
2 tablespoons chopped fresh
  dill or dill seed

zucchini-dill soufflé

Simmer zucchini and lemon juice in boiling salted water to cover
15 minutes. Drain zucchini and set aside. Melt margarine; add
flour and stir in broth. Cook until thickened. Beat egg yolks
and add to sauce. Stir in zucchini and dill. Beat egg whites until
stiff and fold into mixture. Pour into 6-cup prepared soufflé dish.
Preheat oven to 350°F. Place soufflé dish in pan of water and
bake for 50 minutes or until set.

Serves 4.

marshmallow soufflé

Combine squash with margarine and seasonings. Heat through.
In a double boiler, combine marshmallows with milk. Stir until
smooth. Beat egg yolks and add to marshmallows. Combine
marshmallow mixture with squash. Beat egg whites and fold in
gently. Pour into a 4-cup soufflé dish. Preheat oven to 350°F.
and bake 45 minutes. Two tablespoons of an orange flavored
liqueur may be added to the winter squash soufflés just before
folding in egg whites.

Serves 4.

3 cups cooked winter squash
  pulp
2 tablespoons margarine
1/2 teaspoon salt
1/4 teaspoon nutmeg
1/4 teaspoon cinnamon
2 cups miniature or chopped
  marshmallows
1/2 cup milk or cream
3 eggs, separated

squash soufflé

Squash may be baked whole in a 350°F. oven for about an hour. Puncture rind to let steam escape. When cooked, cut open squash and remove seeds and stringy portion. Mash pulp and combine with next six ingredients along with beaten egg yolks. Fold stiffly beaten egg whites into squash mixture. Pour into a greased and floured 6-cup soufflé dish. Bake 40 minutes in a preheated 350°F. oven. May be served with a sauce of orange marmalade and pineapple juice heated or maple syrup and lemon juice.

Serves 6.

4 cups cooked winter squash pulp
4 tablespoons margarine
1/2 teaspoon salt
3 tablespoons brown sugar
1/4 teaspoon nutmeg
1 tablespoon grated orange or lemon peel
Pepper
5 eggs, separated

zucchini soufflé

3 medium zucchini
Salt
1 tablespoon margarine
1 tablespoon flour
1/2 cup milk, scalded
1 teaspoon lemon juice
1/3 cup Gruyère cheese, grated
2 egg yolks
4 egg whites

Cut zucchini into very thin slices crosswise. Spread on paper toweling; sprinkle with salt and allow to drain for a few hours. Rinse and drain dry. Place squash in saucepan with 1/4 cup water. Simmer until transparent. Drain. In saucepan, melt margarine and add flour stirring until smooth. Slowly pour in scalded milk and stir until sauce thickens. Combine zucchini, sauce, lemon juice, and cheese with beaten egg yolks. Beat egg whites until stiff. Gently fold into zucchini mixture. Pour into 4-cup greased and floured soufflé dish. Place soufflé in pan of water and bake at 350°F. for 45 minutes.

Serves 2.

Crêpes

These are thin pancakes onto which a tablespoon of filling is placed. They are then rolled up and served warm with a light sauce such as a béchamel or mornay (see "The Sauce Recipes").

basic batter

    1 cup flour
    ½ teaspoon salt
    ¾ cup milk
    ¾ cup water
    4 eggs
    2 tablespoons margarine, melted

whole wheat batter

    1 cup whole wheat flour
    1 teaspoon salt
    1 cup milk
    ¼ cup bouillon
    4 eggs
    2 tablespoons margarine, melted

Beat all ingredients together in blender. Let stand 1 hour. Thin if necessary. Pour 2 tablespoons batter into greased 6-inch skillet, moderately heated. Tilt pan to spread. Fry until golden brown on each side. They may be frozen for later use. Makes 12-14. Fill these pancakes with one of the fillings below. The crêpes may be the main dish for any meal.

1½ cups zucchini, grated and drained
  2 tablespoons margarine, melted
1½ cups sour cream
1½ cups Parmesan cheese

sour cream filling

Sauté zucchini in margarine until tender. Stir in sour cream and cheese.

cream soup filling

1 cup zucchini, chopped
6 tablespoons onion, chopped
3 tablespoons margarine, melted
1 can condensed cream of chicken or shrimp soup
¼ cup milk

Sauté zucchini and onion in margarine until soft. Stir in soup and milk.

white sauce filling

1 cup béchamel sauce
2 cups mixed vegetables and/or meat

sample combinations

2 tablespoons margarine
¼ cup onion
¼ cup celery
¼ cup mushrooms
½ cup zucchini
¾ cup chopped ham

2 tablespoons margarine
¼ cup celery
¼ cup carrots
¼ cup onion
½ cup zucchini
4 strips bacon, cooked and crumbled

Sauté in margarine the chopped vegetables. Add cooked meat; stir in sauce. Chicken broth may be substituted for the milk and 3 tablespoons grated cheese may be added. *Note:* This is a creative and attractive way to serve leftovers.

Omelets

Like the soufflé, the omelet and its idiosyncracies often strike terror in the heart of a neophyte cook. Some people refuse to meet the challenge and stick to scrambled eggs. There isn't much taste difference; the primary distinctions are texture and appearance.

If the thought of making an omelet throws you, so what? Scramble up some eggs and serve them with one of the following delicious zucchini fillings and who will know the difference?

1 medium zucchini, thinly
   sliced
1 medium onion, sliced
1½ tablespoons olive oil
2 tablespoons water
½ teaspoon fresh basil
¾ cup shredded mild cheese
   Parmesan cheese

zucchini omelet

Simmer zucchini and onion in oil and water until tender. Combine with basil and cheese. Place this mixture inside a 4-egg omelet. Sprinkle with Parmesan.

Serves 2.

spanish squash omelet

Sauté zucchini, green pepper, and onion in oil. Add tomato, Tabasco, seasonings, and ½ the tomato sauce. Simmer 10 minutes. Prepare 4-egg omelet. Remove to platter. Place filling on one-half. Fold and serve with additional sauce.

Serves 2.

1 medium zucchini, thinly
   sliced
2 tablespoons green pepper,
   diced
1 tablespoon onion, diced
1 tablespoon olive oil
1 tomato, peeled, seeded
   and diced
   Dash of Tobasco
   Salt and pepper
1 8-ounce can tomato sauce

Quiches

Borrowing from the inventive French cook again, we discover the quiche or custard pie as a natural for a summer squash dish. The availability of frozen pie shells makes this classic dish a cinch.

zucchini-crumb quiche

Butter a 9-inch pie pan and line with bread crumbs. Cut zucchini into very thin slices. Allow to drain on paper toweling. Sauté squash in olive oil. Drain again on toweling. Melt margarine; add flour. Add scalded milk, stirring until thickened. Stir in cheese, egg, and seasonings. Add zucchini and ladle into prepared pie pan. Bake at 350°F. for 30 minutes or until set.

Serves 4.

1 cup dry bread crumbs
1 medium zucchini
2 tablespoons olive oil
¼ cup margarine
¼ cup flour
⅔ cup milk, scalded
½ cup Romano cheese
1 egg, beaten
¼ teaspoon nutmeg
¼ teaspoon salt
⅛ teaspoon pepper

2 cups zucchini, sliced thin
1 cup onion, sliced
3 tablespoons olive oil
1 clove garlic, minced
1½ teaspoons salt
4 eggs, beaten
1 cup milk
1 cup heavy cream
½ cup Mozzarella, grated
10-inch pie crust

zucchini quiche

Sauté zucchini, onion, and garlic in olive oil. Season with salt. Cover bottom of pie crust with this mixture. Combine remaining ingredients and pour into pie shell. Bake in preheated 375°F. oven 30-35 minutes until custard is set. Serve hot or cold.

Serves 6.

2 cups zucchini or other
  summer squash, thinly
  sliced
1 cup onion, thinly sliced
1 garlic clove, minced
3 tablespoons olive oil
2 teaspoons salt
2 fresh tomatoes, peeled
  and chopped
1 cup tomato sauce
¼ teaspoon oregano
¼ teaspoon tarragon
2 cups cottage cheese (small
  curd)
3 eggs
¾ cup milk
½ cup Mozzarella, grated
  10-inch pie crust

squash quiche italiano

Sauté squash, onion, and garlic in olive oil. Season with salt. Remove. Simmer tomatoes, sauce and remaining seasonings until tomatoes are soft. Mix well cottage cheese, eggs, and milk. Place squash mixture in pie shell. Add egg mixture and 4 table-spoons tomato sauce. Bake 35 minutes in preheated 350°F. oven. Sprinkle on grated Mozzarella and return to oven until cheese melts. Serve quiche with remaining tomato sauce.

Serves 6.

Waffles and Pancakes

Ever have squash or pumpkin for breakfast? There is no time like the present. Tired of your old pancake recipe? Surprise your family and friends at breakfast, brunch, and supper too, with a different kind of pancake or waffle.

zucchini pancakes

Lightly combine all ingredients and allow to rest for ½ hour. Add more milk for a thinner pancake. Cook on lightly greased, hot griddle.

Serves 2-3.

1 medium zucchini, grated and drained
1 egg, beaten
1 tablespoon cooking oil
1 cup pancake mix
¾ cup milk
2 tablespoons Parmesan cheese

squash pancakes

2 cups pumpkin or squash, cooked and mashed
1 cup flour
¼ cup milk
2 tablespoons pancake syrup
¼ teaspoon nutmeg

Combine all ingredients. Cook on hot griddle. Serve with warm syrup.

Serves 2-3.

pumpkin waffles

Sift dry ingredients together. Mix well with eggs, milk, cooking oil, and pumpkin. Stir in nuts. Bake in hot waffle iron. *Note:* Whole wheat flour may be substituted.

Serves 4.

2 cups flour
2 teaspoons baking powder
¼ teaspoon cinnamon
¼ teaspoon ginger
¼ teaspoon nutmeg
½ teaspoon salt
3 eggs, beaten
1¾ cups milk
¾ cup pumpkin pulp, mashed
½ cup cooking oil
½ cup nuts, chopped

Custards

Custard is usually thought of as a type of dessert. This is not necessarily the case. Similar to a quiche, an unsweetened custard is a very suitable base for a vegetable dish. The following recipe is an example. A recipe for a dessert type of custard made with pumpkin is in the section on desserts.

zucchini-rice custard

4 small zucchini, thinly sliced
1/3 cup parsley
1/4 cup rice
1/3 cup flour
1/2 teaspoon salt
1/8 teaspoon cayenne pepper
1 egg
1/4 cup sour cream
1/2 cup Parmesan cheese
2 tablespoons margarine

Cook zucchini in small amount of boiling salted water until tender. Arrange 1/2 the zucchini in 1-quart baking dish. Layer on parsley and rice. Shake remaining zucchini with the flour and place over rice. Stir together the next 4 ingredients and 1/2 the cheese. (A scant cup of milk may replace the sour cream.) Pour custard mixture over all. Dot with margarine and sprinkle with remaining cheese. Bake at 375°F. for 40 minutes or until set.

Serves 4.

zucchini custard pudding

Sprinkle grated zucchini with salt and drain. Before using, squeeze out as much moisture as possible. Beat eggs, add milk, bread crumbs, seasoning, cheese, and melted margarine. Fold in squash. Pour into greased 1-quart oven-proof dish. Bake at 350°F. for 40 minutes.

Serves 4.

1 medium zucchini, grated
1 tablespoon salt
4 eggs
1/2 cup milk or cream
3/4 cup fine dry bread crumbs
1/2 teaspoon oregano
3 tablespoons Parmesan cheese
2 tablespoons margarine, melted

zucchini-cheese puff

Cook zucchini in boiling salted water about 5 minutes. Drain and pat dry. Line a greased 9-inch baking pan with bread slices. Combine zucchini with cheese and margarine. Spread over bread. Beat remaining ingredients and pour over zucchini mix. Refrigerate 1 hour. Bake at 350°F. until puffed, set and browned, 40-50 minutes.

Serves 4.

1 pound zucchini, sliced (about 3 cups)
4 slices cracked wheat bread
8 ounces sharp cheese, shredded
2 tablespoons margarine, softened
3 eggs, beaten
¼ cup onion, minced
½ teaspoon salt
½ teaspoon dry mustard
Cayenne pepper
1½ cups milk

Pickles & Relishes

Pickles & Relishes

Pickling need not be limited to cucumbers especially since cucumbers are tricky to grow and the pickling variety difficult to find in the markets. A lot of people who enjoy pickles and the process of pickling them ought to try putting the good old zucchini in a jar which contains a delicious pickling solution.

Served with cold sandwiches or hamburgers, or added to an antipasto, the versatile zucchini lends itself to several tasty pickling preparations.

grand scale zucchini relish

Prepare zucchini; combine with salt and other vegetables. Allow mixture to stand overnight. Drain; rinse thoroughly and drain again in a colander. Press bowl down on top of vegetable mixture to force out as much liquid as possible. In a large enamel pot, combine remaining ingredients; add vegetables and bring to a rolling boil. Reduce heat and boil gently 20 minutes. Ladle relish into hot sterilized jars and seal.

Makes 8 pints.

10 cups zucchini, minced
1 cup pickling salt
5 cups onion, minced
1 cup celery, diced
3 green peppers, diced
2 sweet red peppers, diced
2 teaspoons turmeric
1 tablespoon dry mustard
3 tablespoons celery seed
6 cups sugar
5 cups white vinegar
3 tablespoons cornstarch

3 quarts zucchini or other
    summer squash
6 cloves garlic
¼ cup pickling salt
2½ cups white vinegar
2½ cups water
3 sprigs fresh dill
3 grape leaves
18 peppercorns

zucchini dill pickles

Cut squash lengthwise into sticks of appropriate size for canning. Combine garlic, salt, vinegar, and water. Bring to a rolling boil. Place two garlic cloves in each hot sterilized jar. Arrange zucchini sticks in jars; add dill and peppercorns, and top with grape leaves. Pour in hot pickling juice. Seal and process in a boiling water bath for 10 minutes.

Makes 3 quarts.

pumpkin pickles

Blanch bite-sized cubes over, not in, boiling water until tender. Combine remaining ingredients and bring to a rolling boil. Reduce heat and simmer 10 minutes. Add pumpkin cubes and simmer an additional 5 minutes. Pack into hot sterilized jars. Seal and process in a boiling water bath for 5 minutes.

Makes 4 pints.

8 cups pumpkin, peeled and
    cubed
2½ cups white vinegar
2½ cups sugar
4 sticks cinnamon
1 teaspoon pickling spices
1 teaspoon cloves

summer squash pickles

Cut squash and onions into thin slices. Combine with salt; mix well and allow to stand for several hours. Combine remaining ingredients and bring to a rolling boil. Squash and onions should be packed in hot sterilized jars. Pour in pickling solution to within ¼ inch of jar top. Seal according to manufacturer's directions and process in a boiling water bath for 15 minutes.

Makes 4 pints.

8 cups summer squash, sliced
2½ cups onion, sliced
1 cup green pepper, diced
1 tablespoon pickling salt
2 cups vinegar
3 cups sugar
1½ teaspoons mustard seed
1 teaspoon celery seed

zucchini bread and butter pickles

1 large onion, sliced
6 cups small squash
¼ cup salt
2 cups cider vinegar
1 cup sugar
1 teaspoon turmeric
1 teaspoon mustard seed
1 teaspoon celery seed

Slice onions and squash ⅛ inch thick and place in a large bowl. Salt thoroughly; cover and allow to rest overnight. Combine remaining ingredients and bring to a rolling boil. Add zucchini and onions to pickling solution. Bring to a boil; reduce heat and simmer 15 minutes. Pack pickles into hot sterilized pint jars. Fill to ½ inch of top with pickling solution. Seal.

Makes 3 pints.

Salads

Salads

Green and yellow summer squash, if they are small and tender, make both colorful and tasty contributions to salad dishes. The dieter, concerned about calorie consumption, can munch away happily on raw vegetables without experiencing any guilt.

Salad dressings, both homemade and commercial, come in such variety that salads of all descriptions and flavors may be served very frequently without fear of boring any palate. Experimenting with additions of mustard seed, dill seed, celery seed, sesame seed, parsley, garlic, or onion salt also will add interest and your own personal touch.

Main dish salads, using almost everything in the garden, can substitute for more expensive entrées which must be purchased at the market. A zucchini Niçoise, for example, makes a mighty filling meal, with or without the optional tuna fish.

zucchini niçoise

Make a salad dressing by combining oil, vinegar, and seasonings. Boil potatoes until done, but not mushy. Place slices in shallow bowl and marinate in some of the dressing. Chill. Cut beans into 2-inch pieces and boil in salted water 15 minutes until tender crisp. Drain, marinate, and chill. Slice zucchini into very thin slices. Marinate and chill. Slice, marinate, and chill onions. Line a salad bowl or serving dish with fresh, crisp lettuce leaves. If tuna is to be included, center it in serving dish, surrounding it with mounds of marinated vegetables. Garnish with tomato and egg wedges. Flavors are enhanced by preparing marinated vegetables several days in advance.

Serves 4.

¾ cup olive oil
¼ cup wine vinegar
¼ teaspoon salt
⅛ teaspoon coarsely ground pepper
4 potatoes, boiled, peeled and sliced
½ pound green beans
1½ pounds zucchini, sliced
Leaf lettuce
1 6½ ounce can tuna
2 medium onions, sliced
2 tomatoes, quartered
2 hardboiled eggs

2 cups small summer
  squash, diced
3 cups shell macaroni,
  cooked
2 cups cabbage, shredded
1 cup carrots, shredded
½ cup green pepper,
  chopped
½ cup red radishes, sliced
3 tablespoons onion, minced
1 cup mayonnaise or sour
  cream
2 tablespoons lemon juice
1½ teaspoons sugar
1½ teaspoons dry mustard
1 teaspoon salt
  Dill seed
  Leaf lettuce

zucchini macaroni salad

Do not peel tender young squash. Combine all ingredients; Mix well. Sprinkle with dill seed. Served chilled on leaf lettuce.

Serves 6.

zucchini and onion in sour cream

Peel squash with potato peeler. Slice very thin. Place on paper toweling to dry for about an hour. Combine all ingredients and mix thoroughly. Refrigerate and serve chilled.

Serves 2-3.

2 cups zucchini, peeled and
  sliced
1 cup onion, sliced
2 tablespoons white vinegar
1 tablespoon white sugar
½ cup sour cream
½ teaspoon dill seed
  Salt and pepper

zucchini salad bowl

Cut squash into very thin slices, or quarter lengthwise and dice, if preferred. Combine with all other ingredients and toss lightly. Serve chilled on a lettuce leaf.

Serves 4.

2 small zucchini, sliced
2 cups cooked potatoes, diced
1 cup cooked peas
1 cup cooked carrots, diced
½ cup onion, chopped
¾ cup sour cream or mayonnaise
1 tablespoon sweet pickle, diced
2 tablespoons vinegar
½ teaspoon salt
⅛ teaspoon pepper
Leaf lettuce

2 cups zucchini, drained and diced
1 cup cooked turnip, diced
1 cup cooked potato, diced
1 cup cooked beets, diced
1 cup cooked peas
French dressing
Mayonnaise
Leaf lettuce or spinach

zucchini salad russe

Combine all vegetables and marinate in French dressing for several hours. Before serving, add enough mayonnaise to bind mixture together. Layer a serving platter with crisp lettuce or spinach leaves. Mound salad in center and garnish with hard-boiled eggs and/or tomato wedges.

Serves 8.

2 envelopes unflavored
  gelatin
½ cup cold water
4 cups tomato juice
1 tablespoon lemon juice
...grated
...il

...diced
...iced or

zucchini-tomato aspic ring

Soften gelatin in cold water. Heat tomato juice; add gelatin and stir until dissolved. Add seasonings and mix well. Allow to cool. Cover bottom of oiled ring mold with ¼-inch layer of gelatin mixture. Place mold in refrigerator and chill until gelatin is set. Place a layer of thin zucchini slices on top of molded gelatin. Layer with ¼ inch liquid gelatin, chill and allow to set. Combine remaining vegetable ingredients. Stir in remaining gelatin; mix well and pour into mold. Chill, unmold and fill ring with cottage cheese, if desired. Sprinkle cheese with paprika.

Serves 8.

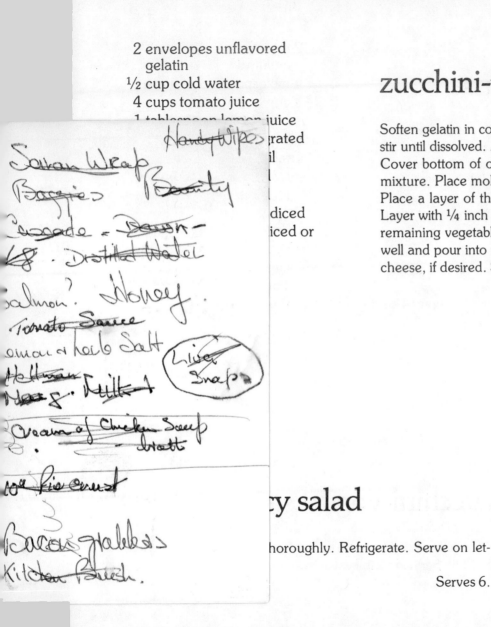

6 cups zucchini, diced
¾ cup green pepper, diced
¼ cup green onion, diced
½ cup salad oil
⅓ cup white vinegar
1 teaspoon sugar
1 envelope spaghetti or taco
  sauce mix
Leaf lettuce

...y salad

...horoughly. Refrigerate. Serve on let-

Serves 6.

zucchini-seafood mousse

If available, use a fish-shaped mold; otherwise either a solid or ring mold is suitable. Soften gelatin in 4 tablespoons cold water. Add boiling water and stir until gelatin is dissolved. Allow mixture to cool. Pour 1/4-inch layer of gelatin into mold and chill until set, then layer zucchini slices on top. Add mayonnaise, lemon juice, salt, and pepper sauce to remaining gelatin mixture. Chill until thickened but not yet firm. Add flaked seafood and minced zucchini; beat well. Whip cream and fold into seafood mixture. Spoon into mold. Chill until firm. Unmold on platter and garnish with tomato wedges and parsley.

Serves 4-6.

2 envelopes unflavored
  gelatin
4 tablespoons cold water
1/2 cup boiling water
1/2 cup zucchini, sliced
1/2 cup mayonnaise
1 tablespoon lemon juice
1 teaspoon salt
  Hot pepper sauce
2 cups salmon or tuna,
  drained
1/2 cup zucchini, minced
1/2 cup whipping cream
  Tomato wedges
  Parsley

1 cup plain yogurt
2 tablespoons olive oil
4 tablespoons fresh mint,
  snipped
4 teaspoons lemon juice
2 cups zucchini, thinly sliced
  and peeled
  Lettuce leaves

zucchini-yogurt salad

Stir together first 4 ingredients. Add zucchini; combine thoroughly. Chill. Serve on lettuce leaves.

Serves 4.

zucchini summer salad

Combine all ingredients except vinegar. Cook over low heat 10 minutes. Vegetables should be tender, but not mushy. Do not overcook. Remove from heat. Add vinegar and toss. Zucchini summer salad may be served hot or chilled.

Serves 6.

2 medium zucchini
6 green onions, chopped
6 stalks celery, chopped
1 green pepper, chopped
1½ tablespoons fresh basil, chopped
½ teaspoon each, rosemary and tarragon
1 teaspoon salt
½ teaspoon pepper
2 medium tomatoes, chopped
2 tablespoons wine vinegar

6 small zucchini
2 avocados, peeled and diced
1 small onion, minced
¼ cup olive oil
1 tablespoon wine vinegar
1 clove garlic, minced
1½ teaspoons salt
¼ teaspoon freshly ground pepper
Leaf lettuce
Tomato wedges

zucchini-avocado salad

Cut squash in half lengthwise. Blanch in boiling salted water 5 minutes. Scoop out pulp and drain shells upside down. Dice squash pulp; combine with diced avocado and onion. Combine oil, vinegar, garlic, salt, and pepper. Mix well. Pour dressing into squash mixture. Spoon into shells and chill thoroughly. Serve on lettuce leaves. Garnish with tomato wedges.

Serves 6-8.

zucchini-stick salad

Slice small squash into sticks. Drain on paper toweling. Place in shallow container and marinate in salad dressing. Serve on lettuce leaves. Decorate with paprika.

Small zucchini or summer squash
Oil and vinegar dressing
Leaf lettuce
Paprika

zucchini oriental salad

Slice and drain squash. Layer in shallow bowl. Mix remaining ingredients in equal parts. Pour over squash. Chill.

Serves 3-4.

3 medium summer squash, sliced
Vinegar
Salad oil
Soy sauce

zucchini-sprout salad

Combine all ingredients. Chill and serve.

Serves 6-8.

2 small zucchini, sliced
1 small yellow squash, sliced
2 cups bean sprouts
1 green pepper, diced
2 tablespoons green onion, chopped
¾ cup French dressing
Salt and pepper

Soups

Soups

Unless we eat at a rather expensive restaurant, few of us dine in such elaborate circumstances as to regard soup as a first course. Informal and economical dining has promoted soup to main course status at both noon and evening meals. "Chewy" or thick soups, not far removed from the stew category, make hearty meals in themselves, usually complemented by French, Italian, or a hearty whole-grain bread. Lighter, more delicate soups, of either a cream or clear variety, served with salad, sandwiches, crackers or whatever may be an appropriate and filling accompaniment, make appetizing luncheon and supper fare.

Homemade vegetable soup will never be outdone by the canned varieties. The cook who prepares soup from scratch knows how wise it is to have frozen vegetables, packaged together or in small separate portions for later combining, to plop in the soup at a moment's notice. In later sections suggested vegetable combinations and packaging for freezing can help you prepare ahead for soups and stews, full of tender and nutritious vegetables to be enjoyed long after the gardening season is over.

This first soup may be served either hot or cold just as you might in the case of Vichyssoise, which is made with potatoes and appears with expected frequency on the dinner menus of most fine restaurants. Squashyssoise may be made of zucchini, crookneck, straightneck or a combination of all three.

squashyssoise (squash soup)

Sauté onions in margarine until translucent. Remove onions and set aside. Sauté squash until soft. Add 1 cup chicken broth. Pour this mixture gradually with onions into blender. Return to saucepan along with remaining broth, milk, and seasonings. Serve hot or cold.

Serves 4.

4 medium onions, minced
2 tablespoons margarine
2 cups summer squash, sliced
4 cups chicken stock or bouillon
1 cup milk or cream
Salt and pepper

cream of squash soup

1 cup onion, minced
2 tablespoons margarine
2½ cups chicken broth
1 cup cooked winter squash
½ teaspoon ground
  cinnamon
¼ teaspoon nutmeg
  Salt and pepper
¾ cup cream or milk
  Croutons, toasted

In a large saucepan, sauté onion in the margarine until tender. Add 1 cup chicken broth and simmer 10 minutes. Gradually pour into blender and blend thoroughly. Return to saucepan. Add squash, remaining broth, and seasonings. Bring to a boil; reduce heat and stir until smooth. Cover and simmer 10 minutes. Add cream. If milk is used, add an additional 2 tablespoons of margarine. Serve with toasted croutons.

Serves 4.

zucchini-spaghetti soup

Sauté onion and garlic in olive oil in large saucepan. Add zucchini rounds, tomato, seasonings, and stock. Cover and simmer over low heat 1½ hours. Add short lengths of uncooked spaghetti and continue simmering another 10 minutes. *Note:* If vegetable stock and vegetable spaghetti are used, this is an all-vegetable dish!

Serves 4.

1 medium onion, minced
1 clove garlic, minced
¼ cup olive oil
1½ pounds small zucchini,
  thinly sliced (4 medium)
1 tomato, peeled and
  chopped
½ teaspoon basil
  Salt and pepper
1 cup vegetable stock or
  chicken broth
½ pound uncooked
  spaghetti or
4 cups vegetable spaghetti
  fibers

creamy squash and corn soup

Sauté onion and garlic in margarine. Add corn and broth. Simmer 10 minutes. Add squash and continue simmering until it begins to disintegrate. Cool, then refrigerate until thoroughly chilled. Before serving, add seasoning to taste and cream. Garnish with parsley.

Serves 6.

1 medium onion, minced
1 clove garlic, minced
2 tablespoons margarine
1½ cups corn
5 cups chicken broth or bouillon
3 cups zucchini, sliced
1 cup chilled cream
Salt and pepper
Fresh parsley, minced

3 ears fresh corn
4 strips bacon
1 pound summer squash, sliced (3 cups)
1 cup onions, minced
¾ cup green pepper, minced
1 garlic clove, minced
1 cup water
1½ teaspoons salt
¼ teaspoon dried basil leaves
¼ teaspoon tarragon
2 cups milk
2 eggs, beaten
Salt and pepper

zucchini-corn chowder

Cut corn from cobs. Sauté bacon until crisp, crumble and set aside. Add zucchini, onions, green pepper, garlic, and sauté in bacon drippings. Add corn, water, and all seasonings. Bring mixture to a boil. Reduce heat and simmer slowly for 10 minutes. Combine milk and eggs. Add to pot and simmer until thickened. Do not allow chowder to boil. Sprinkle on bacon bits.

Serves 6.

¼ cup onion, chopped
1 can cream of chicken
 soup, undiluted
3 cups zucchini, sliced
1¼ cups water, milk or
 chicken broth
 Parsley
 Salt and pepper
 Sour cream

zucchini-chicken soup

Sauté onion in butter until soft. Add next 5 ingredients. Simmer until zucchini is soft. Purée in blender. Chill. Top with a spoonful of sour cream.

Serves 4.

zucchini potage

Sauté zucchini in butter. Combine other ingredients in a saucepan and bring to a boil. Reduce heat and simmer 10 minutes. Add squash and continue cooking until squash begins to disintegrate. Pour mixture into blender and blend thoroughly. Serve with a dollop of sour cream, if desired.

Serves 6.

3 cups zucchini, sliced
1 pint chicken broth or
 bouillon
1 medium onion, sliced
¼ teaspoon chervil
1 cup peas, cooked
 Salt and pepper
 Sour cream for topping

2 small zucchini, grated
1½ cups yogurt
1 clove garlic, minced
1 small onion, minced
2 teaspoons olive oil
2 teaspoons lemon juice
 Salt
 Chopped dill

zucchini-yogurt soup

Combine all ingredients except dill. Chill. When ready to serve, spoon into bowls and top with dill. Thin with dry white wine, if you wish.

Serves 2.

pepper-squash soup

6 strips bacon, cooked and
  crumbled
1 onion, minced
1 clove garlic, minced
1 medium tomato, peeled
  and chopped
2 hot red peppers, minced
2 cups winter squash, peeled
  and cubed
3 cups beef broth or bouillon
¼ teaspoon sugar
  Salt and pepper
  Parmesan cheese for
  topping

Sauté onion and garlic in bacon fat. Drain excess grease. Add tomato and peppers. Simmer until liquid is reduced. Add squash chunks and broth. Bring to boil; reduce heat and simmer 25 minutes. Add seasonings. Serve topped with bacon bits and Parmesan cheese.

Serves 6.

soup in a pumpkin

1 well-shaped 5-pound
  pumpkin
1 cup grated cheese (Mozzarella or Gruyère)
1 cup cooked ham, chopped
2 cups toasted croutons
2 cups cream
  Pinch nutmeg
  Salt and pepper

Remove top of pumpkin. Scoop out seeds and stringy portion. Fill pumpkin with layers of cheese, ham and croutons. Combine cream and seasonings. Pour into pumpkin, adding more cream if necessary to fill shell. Cover with aluminum foil and place pumpkin in baking pan. Heat oven to 325°F. Bake 1½-2 hours, stirring several times. Remove pumpkin from oven; place on large serving dish; top with pumpkin lid and serve soup from pumpkin "bowl."

Serves 4.

Stews

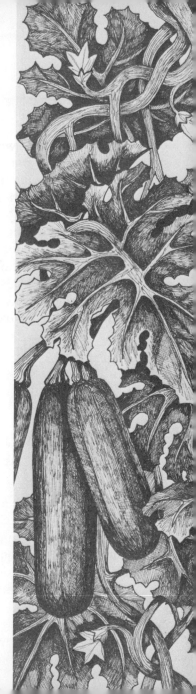

Stews

A stew is a stew, whether it's called a ragout, pot-a-feu, burgoo, goulash, omido, or estofado. The basic principle underlying stew preparation is a successful combination of meat, stock, vegetables, and seasoning.

Zucchini and other summer squash are natural partners with meat and other vegetables. The delicate flavors of green and yellow summer squash join tomatoes, onions, carrots, corn, potatoes, peas, celery, turnips, cauliflower, and beans to produce a delicious vegetarian stew. Veal, pork, beef, chicken, and turkey are all complemented by summer squash. Winter varieties make substantial and tasty contributions to stews and casseroles as well, as you will discover in the recipes which follow. Some of these have been adapted from foreign dishes indigenous to areas and countries in which squash has long been standard fare. Courgettes, marrows, cocozelles, and especially zucchini have been around for a long time in other parts of the world. Isn't it fortunate that gardeners are finally realizing the possibilities these prolific vegetables provide.

zucchini-short rib stew

Brown meat in cooking oil. Add water, salt and pepper. Cover and simmer 2 hours. Skim fat; remove meat and set aside. Add enough water to remaining broth to make 1 cup and set aside. In the pan with additional oil, sauté onion and zucchini until soft. Mix in all ingredients except noodles and simmer gently about 20 minutes. Serve over hot noodles.

Serves 4.

2 pounds short ribs
2 tablespoons cooking oil
1 cup water
  Salt and pepper
1 large onion, chopped
2 cups zucchini, sliced
1 9-ounce can crushed
  pineapple
1 cup tomatoes, peeled and
  chopped
1 8-ounce package egg
  noodles, cooked

6 cups summer squash, sliced
2 tablespoons olive oil
2 tablespoons margarine
3 large onions, sliced
2 large green peppers, chopped
2 celery stalks, diced
2 tomatoes, peeled and quartered
1 tablespoon parsley, chopped
1 tablespoon each basil and
  tarragon
1 clove garlic
  Salt and pepper
  Parmesan cheese

ragout of summer squash

Sauté squash on both sides in oil and melted margarine until soft. Remove. Saute onions, peppers, and celery. Add tomatoes and seasonings. Cook gently 30 minutes. Add squash the last 5 minutes. Sprinkle with cheese.

Serves 4-6.

winter squash-beef stew

Dredge meat in flour. Heat oil in Dutch oven. Brown meat and sauté onion. Add water and seasonings. Reduce heat and simmer 50 minutes. Add potatoes, carrots, and peas; cook 15 minutes more. Add squash and tomato paste and continue cooking for an additional 10 minutes until vegetables are tender.

Serves 6.

3 pounds stew beef
  Flour
2 tablespoons cooking oil
4 medium onions, sliced
2½ cups water
½ teaspoon thyme
½ teaspoon basil
3 medium potatoes
2½ cups carrots, sliced
1½ cup peas
2 cups winter squash, bite-
  sized chunks
½ can tomato paste

stew in a pumpkin

Remove lid of pumpkin and retain for later use. Scoop out seeds and stringy portion. Score inside several times. Rub interior surface with salt and pepper. Place pumpkin upside down in large shallow pan, place lid in pan beside pumpkin. Add ¼-inch water and bake at 350°F for an hour or until it is tender. Remove pumpkin from oven. Drain water and return upright pumpkin to baking pan. Rub inside surfaces with margarine. Dredge meat in flour, brown in oil with garlic. Add onions and simmer until soft. Stir in wine, broth, and seasonings and cook over low heat until meat is tender, about 1 hour. Add all vegetables and simmer 45 minutes. Spoon stew into warm pumpkin. The pumpkin pulp may be eaten with the stew.

Serves 4.

1 well-shaped 5-6 pound pumpkin
Salt and pepper
Margarine
2 pounds stew beef, cut in 1-inch cubes
¼ cup flour
2 tablespoons cooking oil
2 cloves garlic, minced
1 large onion, sliced
1 cup red wine
2 cups beef broth
½ teaspoon salt
½ teaspoon thyme
1 bay leaf
1 cup tomatoes, peeled
2 medium zucchini, sliced
1 can garbanzo beans (20-ounces), drained
2 carrots, sliced
2 potatoes, peeled and cubed

Vegetable Dishes

Vegetable Dishes

No other vegetable, not even the tomato, is as adaptable to so many types of preparation as are squashes. Whether served raw, fresh from the garden, or baked and napped with the most sophisticated sauce, summer squash, zucchini in particular, has no equal in versatility. Winter varieties, although they cannot be recommended in a raw state, are delicious baked, stuffed, mashed, and fried, and therefore, are no slouches either, when it comes to providing interesting and nutritious dishes. Even the squash blossom makes its contribution as you will learn from several of the following recipes.

Whether you are preparing an elegant multi-course dinner of a do-it-yourself cook-out, include some squash on the menu. From appetizer to dessert, there is a squash recipe to fill the bill.

sautéed zucchini halves

Sauté onion in margarine until clear; push to one side. Place zucchini, cut side down, in skillet and cook over low heat until lightly brown. Turn; add remaining ingredients; cover and cook until liquid is almost evaporated. *Note:* A baked stuffed tomato nicely complements the zucchini.

Serves 3.

1 medium onion, thinly sliced
3 tablespoons margarine
3 small zucchini, halved lengthwise
½ teaspoon garlic salt
Few twists freshly ground pepper
½ cup water

3 cups zucchini, sliced ¼-
  inch thick
1 egg, beaten and diluted
  with
2 tablespoons milk
  Cracker crumbs
  Salt and pepper
  Margarine

fried squash slices

Soak zucchini slices in salted water about an hour. Drain on paper toweling. Dip each slice into egg mixture and then into seasoned cracker crumbs. Brown both sides in margarine.

Serves 4.

zucchini sautéed

Sauté first 4 ingredients in margarine and oil about 5 minutes. Add chicken stock and seasonings and simmer 10 minutes.

Serves 2.

2 small zucchini, thinly sliced
1 large onion, thinly sliced
1 clove garlic, minced
½ cup green pepper,
  chopped
2 tablespoons margarine
1 tablespoon oil
⅓ cup chicken stock
  Salt
  Cayenne pepper

fried zucchini parmesan

Fry zucchini and garlic in hot oil until slightly brown. Season and serve sprinkled with parsley and Parmesan.

Serves 2.

1 medium zucchini, sliced
   ½-inch thick
1 small clove garlic, chopped
3 tablespoons hot cooking oil
   Salt and pepper
1 tablespoon parsley,
   chopped
1 tablespoon Parmesan
   cheese

french-fried acorn strips

Fry in deep fat at 360°F. until lightly browned and tender. Drain on paper toweling and sprinkle with seasonings.

Serves 4.

1 medium acorn squash, cut
   into ½-inch thick semi-
   circles, pared
   Brown or granulated sugar
   Allspice

pumpkin fritters

Stir together mashed pumpkin, sugar, flour and vanilla, mixing well. Heat oil to 360°F. Fry spoonfuls of mixture 3-5 minutes. Flatten between sheets of toweling.

Serves 4.

1½ pounds cooked pumpkin,
   mashed and drained
 1 cup sugar
 1 cup flour
 ¾ teaspoon vanilla
 1 cup oil

2 cups ½-inch slices zucchini
or other summer squash
1 cup flour
¾ teaspoon salt
⅛ teaspoon pepper
2 egg yolks, beaten
6 ounces beer
2 tablespoons margarine,
melted
2 egg whites, stiffly beaten

french-fried zucchini

Dry squash slices on paper towels. Combine flour, salt, pepper, egg yolks, and beer. Stir thoroughly. Add melted margarine and let mixture rest 1 hour at room temperature. Fold in egg whites. Dip squash slices into batter and deep fry at 360°F. until browned.

Serves 4.

squash fritters

Mix squash, egg, onion, milk, flour, salt, pepper, and baking powder into batter. Drop batter by the spoonful into hot fat and fry 3-5 minutes until golden brown. Turn each fritter once. Remove to paper toweling.

Serves 4.

1 winter squash or 2 medium
summer squashes, mashed
1 egg, beaten
1 tablespoon onion, minced
2 tablespoons milk
½ cup flour
Salt and pepper
1 teaspoon baking powder
Oil or bacon grease

french-fried butternut

Bake whole squash at 325°F. until peeling softens and can be removed easily. This takes about an hour. Peel squash; slice in half lengthwise and remove seeds. Cut into cubes. Drop squash into deep fat and fry until evenly browned and tender throughout. Drain on paper toweling. Add seasonings.

Serves 4.

1 butternut squash
Cooking oil
Brown sugar or honey
Salt and pepper

1 pound boneless pork,
  cubed
1 tablespoon dry white wine
½ teaspoon salt
¼ teaspoon pepper
2 eggs, beaten
¼ cup flour
4 tablespoons cornstarch
4 cups hot cooking oil
3 cups zucchini, sliced ½-
  inch thick
1 cup carrots, sliced ½-inch
  thick
2 cups small onions, halved
⅓ cup catsup
1 teaspoon soy sauce
¼ cup sugar
¼ cup white vinegar
4 tablespoons oil

zucchini-sweet sour pork

Place meat in bowl and mix well with wine, salt, and pepper. Combine eggs with flour and 3 tablespoons cornstarch. Dip pork cubes into egg mixture and drop into hot cooking oil. Fry in batches until all meat is well-browned. Drain. Prepare and fry vegetables separately in the same manner, allowing about 1 minute cooking time for each. Drain on paper towels. In a bowl combine the additional tablespoon of cornstarch with catsup, soy sauce, sugar, and vinegar. In a separate saucepan heat the additional 4 tablespoons of oil; add above ingredients and stir until thickened. Heat thoroughly with meat and vegetables.

Serves 4.

1 pound pumpkin or winter
    squash, peeled and cut
    into bite-sized cubes
1 cup flour
1/3 teaspoon sugar
1/3 teaspoon salt
1/4 teaspoon cinnamon
1 pinch nutmeg
1 egg, beaten
2 tablespoons vegetable oil
    Hot cooking oil

pumpkin tempura

Dip cubed pumpkin into batter of combined flour, sugar, salt, cinnamon, nutmeg, egg, and vegetable oil and deep fry in hot oil until golden brown. Drain on paper toweling and serve hot.

Serves 4.

zucchini tempura

Dredge squash strips in seasoned flour. Dip into egg mixture and then into bread crumbs. Spread strips on cookie sheet and chill thoroughly. At serving time, fry zucchini in hot fat until browned. Drain briefly on paper toweling and serve immediately.

Serves 6.

6 cups zucchini, sliced in 1/2-
    inch strips
    Salt and pepper
1/3 cup flour
2 eggs, beaten and diluted
    with
1/3 cup milk
1/3 cup dry bread crumbs

zucchini-bean stir-fry

Heat oil in heavy skillet or wok. Stir-fry beans 2-3 minutes, until cooked but still somewhat crisp. Add zucchini, celery, lemon juice, and seasonings. Stir-fry 3 minutes. Add stock; cover and lower heat. Simmer 3 minutes. Moisten cornstarch with 1 tablespoon of the stock; add to mixture. Stir until vegetables are glazed.

Serves 4.

2 tablespoons cooking oil
1 pound fresh green beans, snapped into 2-inch pieces
3 cups zucchini, sliced or chopped
1/4 cup celery, chopped
1 tablespoon lemon juice
1 1/2 teaspoons salt
  Sesame seed
1/3 cup chicken stock or bouillon
1 teaspoon cornstarch

3 tablespoons cooking oil
1 clove garlic, minced
3 cups zucchini, sliced
4 cups cabbage, grated
1 medium onion, sliced
2 teaspoons salt
1 teaspoon sugar
  Pepper
  Celery seed

zucchini-cabbage stir-fry

Heat oil in wok; add garlic; brown and discard. Add vegetables and stir-fry 2-3 minutes. Add seasonings; reduce heat and continue stirring 5-6 minutes until vegetables are cooked but still crisp.

Serves 6.

zucchini-chicken stir-fry

Heat oil in skillet or wok. Stir-fry squash until tender, but crisp. Remove squash and set aside. Add chicken and mushrooms and stir-fry 2 minutes over high heat. Season with salt and pepper. Remove from wok and set aside on warm platter with zucchini. Pour soy sauce and wine into wok and stir 2 minutes until sauce is slightly thickened. Pour over zucchini-chicken mixture.

Serves 4.

3 tablespoons cooking oil
1 medium zucchini, cut into strips
1 pound cooked, boned chicken, strips cut $1/4$-inch thick
$1/2$ pound fresh mushrooms, sliced
$1/2$ teaspoon salt
Lemon-flavored pepper
$1 1/2$ tablespoons soy sauce
$1/3$ cup dry white wine or Vermouth

2 tablespoons cooking oil
$1/2$ cup green pepper strips
$1/2$ cup carrot strips
$1/2$ cup celery strips
1 medium zucchini, cut into thin strips
2 tablespoons chicken broth
6 ounces snow peas
Salt and pepper

stir-fry vegetable strips

Stir-fry thin green pepper and carrot strips in hot oil 1 minute. Add celery and zucchini. Stir-fry 1 minute. Add chicken broth; cover and cook 30 seconds. Add snow peas and cook 1 minute more. Season.

Serves 6.

zucchini charcoal-grilled

Wrap each vegetable in buttered heavy-duty aluminum foil. Place foil package on coals to bake. Potatoes need about 40 minutes, rest of vegetables 20 minutes. They can be baked together by starting the potatoes first. Turn package once during baking.

Zucchini, crookneck or other summer squash, sliced
Tomatoes, quartered
Green peppers, quartered
Small onions
New potatoes
Salt and pepper

hash browns

Sausage grease or bacon fat
Potatoes, diced
Apples, chopped
Butternut, diced

Peel potatoes, apples, and butternut squash. Then fry, chopped, in any proportion, in hot fat.

zucchini-pork chops in foil

Cut squares of heavy-duty aluminum foil. Place vegetables and seasonings on a pork chop in the center of each square. Join 4 corners of foil square and twist top to close packages. Grill over coals 50-60 minutes, never allowing fire to flame. Foil packages may also be placed in 350°F. oven about an hour.

Serves 4.

3 medium zucchini, sliced
2 medium onions, sliced
3 carrots, sliced
Salt and pepper
4 center cut pork chops

3 medium zucchini, sliced
3 medium tomatoes, sliced
1 green pepper, sliced
1 envelope onion soup mix
¼ cup margarine, softened
1 tablespoon brown sugar
¼ teaspoon salt
  Pepper

foil-wrapped zucchini

Cut a large square of heavy-duty aluminum foil. Mix all ingredients and place on square. Fold up securely so no juices escape. Place on charcoal grill, turning once during a 35-40-minute cooking period. Package may be placed in 350°F. oven.

Serves 6.

zucchini stew in foil

Combine all ingredients in large bowl and mix well. Prepare 6 18-inch squares of heavy-duty aluminum foil. Divide stew into 6 equal portions and spoon into foil. Season well. Join 4 corners of each square and twist top of bundles to seal. Refrigerate until fire is suitable for cooking. An even fire of hot gray coals is preferable to a red hot one. Grill for 50-60 minutes, never allowing fire to flame. This is a great camping dish since stew may be served in foil packages, and there are no dishes to wash. *Note:* This stew may be made without meat. Simple increase amount of vegetables.

Serves 4.

2 pounds stew beef, cubed
2 medium zucchini, sliced
4 potatoes, peeled and
  cubed
2 onions, sliced
4 carrots, sliced ¼-inch thick
2 cans condensed mush-
  room soup
  Salt and pepper

butternut squash kebobs

Scrub vegetables and apples. Do not peel. Cut squash in half; remove seeds and stringy portion. Cut into chunks. Leave turnips whole. Combine on skewers. Halve or quarter sweet potatoes. Quarter and core apples. Alternate on skewers. Grill apples and sweet potatoes, brushed with butter, 30-40 minutes; squash and turnips 25 minutes. If preferred, vegetables and apples may be combined in aluminum foil packages to which pats of butter have been added.

Butternut squash
Small turnips
Sweet potatoes
Apples

2 medium acorn squash, cut
  crosswise 1-inch thick
1 pound pork sausage
1 medium onion, chopped
1 green pepper, chopped
½ cup soft bread crumbs
1 egg, beaten
  Seasoned pepper
  Parslied garlic salt

acorn squash rings in foil

Place each ring on a square of foil. Combine remaining ingredients. Place in center of each ring. Dot with margarine, if desired. Seal tightly. Bake at 350°F. for 1 hour. *Note:* Substitute Italian sausage or ground beef. You also may use stuffing with cooked meat to fill acorn squash halves. Bake squash halves 30 minutes; fill and bake 30 minutes more.

Serves 4.

zucchini shashlik

Marinate vegetables in Italian or other oil-vinegar dressing for at least an hour. Arrange vegetables on skewers. Grill over charcoal about 20 minutes.

Serves 4.

1 medium green zucchini, cut into chunks
1 medium golden zucchini or other yellow summer squash, cut into chunks
8 cocktail tomatoes
1 green pepper, cut into small squares
4 medium onions, quartered
1 cup salad dressing

4 medium zucchini
1 large onion, chopped
1 clove garlic, diced
4 tomatoes, peeled and chopped
½ cup green pepper, chopped
1 tablespoon oil
4-6 ounces cooked meat, ground, or chopped or 3 slices bacon, fried crisp and crumbled
Salt and pepper
4 ounces bread crumbs
4 ounces Parmesan or Cheddar, grated

zucchini stuffed with ground meat

Simmer zucchini in boiling salted water about 12 minutes. Cut lengthwise; scoop out pulp and chop. Combine pulp, onion, garlic, tomatoes, green pepper, oil, meat, and seasonings. Pile mixture into zucchini halves and place on baking sheet. Top with bread crumbs and grated cheese. Bake in 375°F. oven approximately 15 minutes. *Note:* The proportions in this basic stuffing recipe may be altered to fit the size of the zucchini or the amount of ingredients you have on hand.

Serves 8.

spinach-squash boats

Halve zucchini lengthwise and simmer in boiling salted water until barely tender. Scoop out pulp; dice and add to chopped spinach. Cook bacon and sauté onion in bacon grease. If leftover chopped ham is used, sauté it with onion in small amount of margarine. Combine all ingredients and fill shells. Bake in 375° F. oven for 20 minutes.

Serves 4.

2 medium zucchini
1 cup cooked spinach, chopped
½ cup diced ham or 4 strips bacon
1 tablespoon onion, minced
2 tablespoons flour
½ cup milk
½ cup Mozzarella, shredded
Salt and pepper

2 cups water
¾ cup white vinegar
3 tablespoons sugar
1 bay leaf
1 celery stalk with leaves
¼ teaspoon coriander
¼ teaspoon salt
Pepper
2 medium summer squash
1½ cups cooked fish, flaked (cod, halibut, turbot, etc.)
1 small onion, minced
2 teaspoons lemon juice
½ cup sour cream
¼ teaspoon basil

fish stuffed squash

Combine in a saucepan water, vinegar, sugar, bay leaf, celery, coriander, salt, and pepper. Bring to a rolling boil; reduce heat and simmer for 8 minutes. Slice squash lengthwise. Cover with prepared liquid and simmer until almost tender. Scoop out pulp. Turn shells upside down to drain. Combine pulp, fish, minced onion, lemon juice, and sour cream. Season. Fill squash with mixture. Chill thoroughly. Serve on lettuce leaf with tomato wedges as garnish, if desired.

Makes 4.

zucchini-tuna boats

Split squash lengthwise and scoop out centers (use with other fresh vegetables in a salad). Combine remaining ingredients and fill shells.

Makes 6.

3 young, tender zucchini
1 7-ounce can of tuna
½ cup Cheddar or American cheese, shredded
½ cup diced celery
2 eggs, hardboiled and chopped
⅓ cup mayonnaise or sour cream
2 tablespoons sweet pickle, minced
1 tablespoon onion, minced

6 squash
6 strips bacon
1 medium onion, minced
2 cloves garlic, minced
1 cup dry bread crumbs
1 tablespoon parsley, minced
¼ teaspoon basil
¼ teaspoon tarragon
¼ teaspoon rosemary
Salt and pepper
½ cup chicken broth or bouillon

stuffed pattypan

Cut thin lids from squash. Blanch squash and lids 10-15 minutes until tender. Scoop pulp from squash and chop. Turn squash upside down to drain. Sauté bacon, drain and crumble. Sauté onion and garlic in bacon drippings. Pour off excess grease; add bread crumbs, squash pulp, and seasonings. Simmer 5 minutes. Add crumbled bacon. Butter squash cases and stuff with mixture. Place squash in shallow baking dish; add broth. Top squash with lids. Bake at 350°F. about 20 minutes.

Serves 6.

acorn squash with green beans

Bake acorn squash cut side down 45 minutes at 350°F. Fill with green beans. Cream remaining ingredients and spoon over top. Heat 15 minutes more.

Serves 2.

1 acorn squash, cut in half lengthwise and seeded
1 cup green beans, cooked
1/3 cup margarine, softened
2 tablespoons onion, minced
Parslied garlic salt
Pinch of basil and oregano
Few drops lemon juice
Freshly ground black pepper

1 medium acorn squash, cut in half lengthwise
Salt
1 cup onion, chopped
2 tablespoons margarine
1 tablespoon flour
1/2 cup milk
Nutmeg to taste

acorn squash with scalloped onions

Remove seeds from squash halves and place cut side down on cookie sheet. Bake in 350°F. oven for 45 minutes. With fork loosen pulp a little and salt well. Cook chopped onion in boiling salted water until tender; drain. In saucepan melt margarine; stir in flour and gradually add milk until thickened. Combine with onion and pour into squash halves. Sprinkle on nutmeg and return to oven for 15 minutes.

Serves 2.

acorn squash entrée

Bake squash halves, cut side down, on baking sheet in a 350°F. oven for 45 minutes. Meanwhile prepare filling. In a saucepan melt margarine; stir in garlic and flour. Gradually add milk and stir until thickened. Sauté green pepper and onion in bacon fat until soft. Combine all ingredients with peeled, chopped and drained tomatoes. Spoon into squash and return to oven for 15 minutes.

Serves 2.

1 medium-large acorn squash, cut in half lengthwise
3-4 slices bacon, cooked crisp and crumbled
1 tablespoon margarine
1 clove garlic, minced
1½ tablespoons flour
½ cup milk
¼ cup green pepper, diced
¼ cup onion, chopped
Salt
Oregano
1 cup ripe tomatoes

sweet baked acorn squash

1 medium acorn squash, halved lengthwise
1 tablespoon margarine, melted
¼ cup milk
¼ cup maple syrup

Scoop out seeds and stringy portion of squash. Place cut side down on cookie sheet. Bake in 350°F. oven 45 minutes. Turn; fill with remaining ingredients and bake another 15 minutes. *Note:* Other sweeteners for this popular recipe are brown sugar, currant jelly, crushed pineapple, mint jelly, applesauce, apple butter, or chutney. Omit the milk with these.

Serves 2.

acorn squash filled with mixed vegetables

Bake squash as in preceding recipe. Fill with mixed vegetables and white sauce or a more piquant sauce made by combining the remaining ingredients.

Serves 2.

1 acorn squash, cut in half lengthwise
1 cup mixed vegetables (succotash; peas and carrots; green pepper, celery and corn; peas, onions and mushrooms; etc.)
½ cup white sauce or
3 tablespoons yogurt
3 tablespoons mayonnaise
2 tablespoons buttermilk
Chopped herbs
Garlic salt

toasted almond squash

Cook squash in boiling salted water until tender. Scoop out pulp and beat pulp with margarine until smooth. Stir in syrup and nutmeg. Fill squash cases with this mixture and top with slivered toasted almonds. Bake in 350°F. oven until heated through. *Note:* A 1-quart casserole may be substituted for the squash shells if more convenient.

Serves 2.

1 medium butternut, cut in half lengthwise
3 tablespoons margarine
½ cup maple syrup
Dash of nutmeg
⅓ cup toasted almonds

2 acorn squash, cut in half
   lengthwise
½ cup celery, diced
½ cup carrot, diced
2 tablespoons onion, diced
1 tablespoon margarine
1 cup cooked ham, diced or
   4-5 strips bacon, cooked
Salt
Broth or milk

mashed acorn squash stuffed

Bake squash until tender at 350°F. Sauté vegetables in margarine until soft; stir in meat. Remove seeds from squash; scoop out pulp and mash with salt and enough broth or milk to make a fluffy texture. Combine with vegetable mixture; pack into squash dishes and bake an additional 15 minutes.

Serves 4.

pumpkin cider bowl

Cut lid from pumpkin; scoop out seeds and stringy portion. Score interior several times. Place pumpkin and lid upside down in large shallow pan. Add ¼-inch water and place in preheated oven at 350°F. Reduce heat to 300°F. and bake 30 minutes. Remove and rub interior with margarine. Allow to cool. Heat remaining ingredients until sugar or honey is dissolved. Pour mixture into pumpkin and reheat until pumpkin is done. Serve from the "cider bowl" by scooping out the cider-laced pulp. Greater amounts of cider may be used and served as a drink; the pulp eaten later.

1 5- or 6-pound edible
   pumpkin
   Margarine
½ cup sugar or honey
½ cup apple cider
1 cinnamon stick
¼ teaspoon nutmeg

fruit-filled winter squash

Cut squashes in half and remove lids. Simmer, cut side down, in 1-inch water in covered skillet until tender. Chop fruit and simmer with sweetener. Fill squash halves. Heat in 350°F. oven until warmed through, about 10 minutes. *Note:* Fresh fruit may be used by combining 1 cup orange sections, 1 tablespoon grated orange peel, ½ cup grapefruit sections, and 2 tablespoons raisins with brown sugar in buttered squash half, cooked. Bake 15 minutes at 375°F.

Serves 4.

2 acorn or other winter squash
4 each dried apples, apricots, peaches, and prunes (or an equal amount of 2)
2 tablepsoons honey or sugar syrup

4 zucchini (1¼-1½ pounds)
2 tablespoons onion, chopped
1 tablespoon margarine
½ cup seasoned stuffing
¼ cup toasted wheat germ
1 small tomato, peeled and chopped
¼ cup grated cheese

wheat germ-stuffed zucchini

Blanch zucchini until barely tender. Cut in half lengthwise. Scoop out pulp. Brown onion in margarine. Chop zucchini pulp with stuffing, wheat germ, and tomato. Add mixture to skillet and simmer until reduced. Stuff shells and sprinkle with grated cheese. Bake in 350°F. oven until cheese melts.

Serves 4.

stuffed zucchini mornay

Make a sauce in a saucepan by melting 2 tablespoons margarine and adding flour. Stir in milk and mix well. Beat egg yolk
and cream together; add 2 tablespoons of sauce. Combine this
mixture with remaining sauce in saucepan and stir till heated
through. Add Gruyère and stir until melted. Cut squash in half
lengthwise and blanch in boiling water 5 minutes. Drain. Scoop
out pulp and ham. Combine with sauce and season to taste.
Fill squash shells; sprinkle with Parmesan and bake at 400°F.
until cheese is melted.

Serves 6.

2 tablespoons margarine
2 tablespoons flour
1 cup milk
1 egg yolk
2 tablespoons cream
2 tablespoons Gruyère
  cheese, grated
  Salt and pepper
3 medium squash
½ cup onion, minced
2 tablespoons margarine
½ cup cooked ham, minced
  or crumbled bacon bits
2 tablespoons Parmesan
  cheese, grated

3 medium zucchini
¼ cup vegetable oil
2 tablespoons vinegar
2 tablespoons sugar
  Chopped sweet basil to
  taste
  Salt and pepper

zucchini sweet and sour

Cut zucchini into ½-inch rounds or strips. Sauté in oil until
lightly brown and soft; remove. Add remaining ingredients to
pan and simmer 3 minutes. Season.

Serves 4.

zucchini stuffed in tomatoes

Sauté bread crumbs, garlic and onions in margarine. Combine in a bowl with seasonings, egg, wine, zucchini, and tomato pulp. Stuff tomatoes and place in a shallow baking dish. Bake at 375°F. for 20 minutes.

Serves 4.

2 tablespoons bread crumbs
½ clove garlic, minced
¼ cup onions, chopped
2 tablespoons margarine
1 teaspoon salt
⅛ teaspoon cayenne pepper
¼ teaspoon oregano
¼ teaspoon dill seed or celery seed
1 egg, beaten
1 tablespoon dry white wine
3 small zucchini, grated and drained
4 large firm tomatoes, insides reserved

baby buttered zucchini

Halve squash lengthwise and cook until tender in lightly salted water. To serve place squash on individual plates; top with sautéed onion rings and nap with sauce of garlic salt and melted butter.

Serves 4.

8 small zucchini
1 medium onion
Garlic salt
2 tablespoons butter

1 medium zucchini or cocozelle, thinly sliced
1 medium yellow summer
squash, thinly sliced
(crookneck, golden zuc-
chini or straightneck)
2 tablespoons margarine
¼ teaspoon salt
¼ teaspoon pepper
1 cup cream
½ teaspoon fresh dill or
¼ teaspoon dill seed

green and yellow zucchini in cream

Drain squash slices on paper toweling. Sauté in melted margarine. Season with salt and pepper. Add cream and simmer mixture over low heat for 15 minutes. Mix well with dill. Serve hot.

Serves 4.

zucchini au gratin

Cut zucchini lengthwise and into slices ¼-inch thick. Melt 1 tablespoon margarine in a skillet; stir in bread crumbs; toss and set
aside. Melt remaining margarine and sauté sliced squash 3-5
minutes. Add remaining ingredients to skillet and heat until
cheese is melted. Serve topped with crumbs.

Serves 6.

2 medium zucchini
2 tablespoons margarine
¼ cup dry bread crumbs
½ can condensed cream of
mushroom soup
⅓ cup Cheddar or American
cheese, shredded
1 tablespoon onion, minced
Salt and pepper

garden medley

Sauté onion and garlic in oil in deep skillet. Add remaining ingredients; cover and simmer 20 minutes.

Serves 6.

1 onion, minced
1 clove garlic, minced
3 tablespoons olive oil
2 beets, sliced
1 green pepper, chopped
2 medium zucchini, sliced
2 cups cabbage, shredded
1 tomato, peeled and seeded
1 teaspoon rosemary
1 teaspoon thyme
½ cup water

1 medium zucchini
1 tablespoon salt
3 tablespoons olive oil
1 clove garlic, minced
¼ teaspoon oregano
¼ teaspoon dried parsley flakes
¾ pound spaghetti, linguini, etc.
Parmesan cheese

zucchini with pasta

Peel squash and cut into julienne strips. Salt thoroughly and place in strainer to drain. Pat dry with paper toweling. Heat olive oil and sauté zucchini and garlic; add seasonings. Cook pasta according to package directions; drain and arrange on serving platter or individual serving dishes. Spoon zucchini mixture onto hot pasta. Sprinkle with Parmesan cheese.

Serves 2.

south of the border squash

Sauté squash, onion, and peppers in oil till soft. Add tomatoes, corn and water. Simmer 10-12 minutes. Season.

Serves 4-6.

2 zucchini, sliced (2 cups)
2 golden zucchini, sliced (2 cups)
1 medium onion, minced
2 green peppers, minced
¼ cup olive oil
1 tomato, peeled and chopped
2 cups yellow corn
½ cup water
Salt and pepper

2 tablespoons olive oil
½ cup onion, chopped
1 clove garlic, minced
2 medium zucchini, sliced
1 small green pepper, chopped
2 tomatoes, peeled and chopped
2 teaspoons salt
¼ teaspoon black pepper
¼ teaspoon oregano
Cheese (optional)

zucchini provençal

Heat oil in skillet and cook onion and garlic for 5 minutes. Add remaining ingredients and cook until most of the liquid has evaporated. *Note:* This mixture may be placed in a shallow casserole; extended with ½ cup cooked rice, and topped with a layer of cheese. Heat in moderate oven until cheese is melted. Experiment with various other herbs such as basil, savory, rosemary, or thyme.

Serves 4.

zucchini succotash

Heat oil and sauté garlic and onion. Add remaining ingredients. Season and simmer covered for 20 minutes. Sprinkle with paprika, if desired.

Serves 6.

½ cup olive oil
1 clove garlic, minced
2 tablespoons onion, minced
2 cups zucchini, diced
2 cups corn
2 cups cooked lima beans
1 green pepper, minced
1 red sweet pepper, minced
Salt and pepper

1 medium butternut, cut into cubes
Salt and pepper
2 tablespoons margarine
1 tablespoon tarragon
1 tablespoon parsley

simple butternut

Cook squash in boiling water 10 minutes. Drain and peel. Toss with remaining ingredients.

Serves 4.

zucchini plus yogurt

Sauté zucchini rounds in oil. Drain and season. Arrange on plates. Combine remaining ingredients and spoon over zucchini.

Serves 4.

3 medium zucchini, sliced ¼-inch thick
½ cup olive oil
¼ teaspoon salt
¼ teaspoon black pepper
8 ounces plain yogurt
½ teaspoon green onion or chives

zucchini español

Slice zucchini and sauté in oil with onion, green pepper, and garlic until tender. Add tomatoes and simmer 10 minutes until liquid has been reduced. Add olives and seasoning. Continue simmering for 15 minutes.

Serves 6.

4 medium squash (1½ pounds)
¼ cup olive oil
1 medium onion, minced
1 green pepper, minced
2 cloves garlic, minced
4 tomatoes, peeled and chopped
1 cup black olives, pitted and chopped
1 tablespoon basil
1 teaspoon oregano
Salt and pepper

¼ cup margarine
2 medium onions, minced
2 cloves garlic, minced
2 teaspoons curry powder
1¼ teaspoon ground cumin
1 teaspoon salt
2 cups zucchini, diced
2 cups small cauliflower florets
1½ cups carrot rounds
1½ cups chicken broth or bouillon
1 tablespoon lemon juice

zucchini curry

In margarine sauté onion and garlic. Add seasonings. Add remaining vegetables and stock. Cook 20 minutes. Add lemon juice.

Serves 4.

baked squash and onions au gratin

Bake squash or pumpkin wedges at 350°F. about 40 minutes. Steam onions on a rack over boiling water 30 minutes. Melt margarine; mix with flour and gradually add milk. Blend in cheese and seasonings, stirring continually. Spoon hot sauce and onions over squash wedges.

Serves 4.

Winter squash or pumpkin
   wedges to serve 4
10 small or 5 medium onions,
   steamed
 1 tablespoon margarine
 1 tablespoon flour
¾ cup milk
½ cup grated cheese
   Salt, pepper and paprika

1 cup butternut, mashed
1 cup sweet potatoes,
   mashed
¼ cup margarine, softened
½ teaspoon salt
¼ teaspoon nutmeg
¼ teaspoon cinnamon
⅛ teaspoon black pepper

butternut and sweet potatoes mashed

Whip all ingredients together until fluffy. For flavor variations, try mint, cloves, ginger, poppy, or sesame seed, bits of orange or lemon peel, and grated apple.

Serves 4.

2 acorn squash, cut in half
    lengthwise, seeds removed
¼ cup margarine, melted
¼ cup light molasses
¼ teaspoon salt
¼ teaspoon nutmeg
    Chopped walnuts

candied winter squash

Fill prepared squash halves with rest of ingredients. Place in baking dish. Cover and bake at 350°F. for 1 hour.

Serves 4.

baked pumpkin

Bake wedges at 350°F. until pulp is soft. Remove skin from pulp; mash with remaining ingredients according to preferences of flavors and consistency. Serve on toast or English muffins.

1 pumpkin, cut into wedges
    Honey
    Nutmeg
    Seedless raisins
    Salt

candied pumpkin

1 small pumpkin or medium
    winter squash
¾ cup margarine, melted
⅓ cup brown sugar
¼ cup preserved ginger,
    chopped

Cut pumpkin or squash into wedges large enough for an individual serving. Lightly grease a large baking dish and place squash in, skin side down. Stir sugar and ginger in margarine over low heat until sugar is dissolved. Ladle over squash and bake, covered, until tender, approximately 1 hour at 350°F.

Serves 4.

basic zucchini casserole

In a greased 1-quart baking dish layer zucchini, tomatoes, and onions until used up. Sprinkle each zucchini layer with salt and pepper and dot with margarine. Sprinkle crumbs on top. Bake uncovered at 350°F. until vegetables are done.

Serves 2.

1 medium zucchini, thinly sliced
1 medium tomato, peeled and chopped or sliced
1 medium onion, sliced thinly
Salt and pepper
Margarine
½ cup bread crumbs

¼ teaspoon garlic salt
1 teaspoon Italian seasoning or
1 teaspoon of oregano, basil, savory, or rosemary or a combination of these herbs equal to 1 teaspoon
See basic recipe above.

basic zucchini casserole plus herbs

Sprinkle herbs on the zucchini layers.

basic zucchini casserole plus cheese

Add a layer of cheese inside the basic casserole and one on top. Then sprinkle with bread crumbs.

6 ounces Muenster, Mozzarella, Cheddar, Gruyère, Swiss, American, Romano, or Parmesan, grated or sliced
See basic recipe above.

squash oriental

Bake squash halves 30 minutes at 375°F. Combine other ingredients. Fill squash halves with ginger mixture and bake for 25 minutes or until squash is done.

Serves 4.

2 acorn squash or small pumpkins, cut in half lengthwise
1½ tablespoons margarine, melted
1½ tablespoons light brown sugar
1 tablespoon sherry
¼ teaspoon ginger
Salt and pepper

1 medium zucchini, diced
1 medium eggplant, peeled and diced
2 tablespoons olive oil
½ pound ground beef
1 can tomato paste
¼ cup onion, chopped
¼ cup green pepper, chopped
1 clove garlic, minced
1 teaspoon salt
½ teaspoon pepper
½ cup dry red wine
½ cup sour cream
1 8-ounce can tomato sauce
1 cup Mozzarella cheese, shredded

basic zucchini casserole gourmet

Sauté zucchini and eggplant in oil; add ground beef and brown. Stir in next 8 ingredients and heat thoroughly. Turn into 1½-quart greased baking dish and top with tomato sauce and cheese. Bake 45 minutes at 350°F.

Serves 2.

basic zucchini parmigiana

Simmer tomatoes, tomato paste, and olive oil 25 minutes. Sauté zucchini in oil until soft. Combine seasoned bread crumbs, parsley, Parmesan, and garlic. In a greased 1½-quart baking dish layer ½ the zucchini, bread mixture, tomato sauce, and Mozzarella. Repeat. Bake 15 minutes at 350°F.

Serves 4.

2½ cups tomatoes
3 tablespoons tomato paste
¼ cup olive oil
2 medium zucchini, sliced ½-inch thick
2 cups bread crumbs, seasoned with
1 tablespoon basil, salt and pepper
2 tablespoons parsley
⅓ cup grated Parmesan
1 large clove garlic, chopped
8 ounces Mozzarella, sliced

1 cup zucchini, coarsely grated and drained
1 cup carrot, grated
3 eggs
1 cup onion, chopped
⅓ cup dill
½ cup mint leaves, chopped
½ cup parsley, snipped
1 cup Muenster, grated
½ cup Feta, mashed
Salt, pepper and paprika
1½ cups flour

zucchini cheese squares

Place all ingredients in a large bowl, mixing well with flour. Turn into a well-greased 9-inch square baking dish. Bake for 50 minutes at 350°F. until browned. Cut into squares.

Serves 6.

zucchini-barley casserole

Add barley to boiling salted water. Reduce heat and simmer for 45 minutes. Meanwhile cook the vegetables in oil until tender. Combine with barley; season and place in a 1-quart greased casserole. Top with cheese and bake for 20 minutes at 350°F.

Serves 2-3.

1 cup barley (or bulghur)
2 cups water
1 small onion, minced
1 small clove garlic, minced
1/2 cup green pepper, chopped
1/2 cup celery, chopped
1 tomato, peeled and chopped
2 small zucchini, chopped
1 tablespoon olive oil
1/4 teaspoon Italian seasoning
3/4 cup grated Cheddar cheese

3 medium squash, sliced 1/2-inch thick
1/2 cup onion, diced
1 tablespoon margarine
2 cups fresh corn, cooked
2 eggs, beaten
1 cup Mozzarella cheese, shredded
1/2 teaspoon salt
Pepper
1/2 cup fine bread crumbs, buttered

zucchini-corn combo

Simmer squash in boiling salted water until tender. Drain and mash. Sauté onion in margarine and combine squash, corn, eggs, cheese, and seasonings. Pour mixture in a 1 1/2-quart greased baking dish and top with buttered crumbs. Bake for 35-40 minutes at 350°F.

Serves 4.

zucchini and cheese

Add cheeses to eggs and seasonings. Steam zucchini and onion till soft; drain and mash. Combine with egg mixture in a 1-quart greased casserole. Bake for 30 minutes at 325°F. *Note:* To increase the consistency, add ⅓ cup crushed crackers.

Serves 2.

½ cup Swiss cheese, grated
⅓ cup Cheddar cheese, grated
2 eggs, beaten
1 teaspoon basil
Salt and pepper
1½-2 cups zucchini, chopped
¼ cup onion, chopped
Buttered bread crumbs

4 medium zucchini, sliced ½-inch thick
⅓ cup onion, chopped
6 tablespoons margarine, melted
1 cup sour cream
1 can condensed cream of chicken soup
1 cup shredded carrot
2 cups seasoned bread crumbs

zucchini with chicken soup

Sauté zucchini and onion in 4 tablespoons margarine until tender. Combine first 6 ingredients with 1½ cups bread crumbs in a 1½-quart greased casserole. Sprinkle with remaining crumbs tossed with 2 tablespoons margarine. Bake for 30 minutes at 350°F. *Note:* Substitute cream of shrimp or mushroom soup with chopped green peppers, or try 2 cups cooked and mashed winter squash instead of zucchini.

Serves 6.

1 clove garlic, minced
2 medium onions, minced
2½ tablespoons olive oil
2 green peppers, sliced
1 small eggplant, peeled and
  diced
2 medium zucchini, sliced
1 cup tomatoes, peeled and
  seeded or equivalent
  tomato sauce
  Salt and pepper
1 baked pie shell
  Parmesan cheese
  Olive oil

zucchini tart niçoise

Sauté garlic and onion in olive oil. Add next 5 ingredients and simmer until liquid is almost evaporated and vegetables are tender, about 45 minutes. Spoon into baked pie shell and heat in moderate oven 10 minutes. Top with cheese and a little olive oil; heat for 5 minutes more.

Serves 6.

hubbard squash casserole

Mix squash pulp with 2 tablespoons margarine, brown sugar, ¼ cup crumbs, mustard and seasonings. Place in baking dish. Top with remaining margarine and crumbs. Bake about 20 minutes at 350°F.

Serves 2.

1 cup cooked squash,
  mashed
¼ cup margarine, melted
2 tablespoons brown sugar
½ cup cracker crumbs
1 tablespoon prepared
  mustard
1 egg, slightly beaten
  Salt and pepper

sweet baked winter squash

In a bowl combine margarine, eggs, sugar, nuts, coconut, orange juice, salt, and vanilla. Pour mixture into casserole and stir squash in thoroughly. Bake for 30 minutes at 350°F. Top with marshmallows and bake until topping turns golden.

Serves 6.

6 tablespoons margarine, melted
3 eggs, beaten
½ cup brown sugar
½ cup chopped pecans or hickory nuts
½ cup coconut, flaked
½ cup orange juice
½ teaspoon salt
½ teaspoon vanilla
2½ pounds winter squash, cooked and mashed
1 cup tiny marshmallows

2 cups sweet potato squash, cooked, peeled, and mashed
3 tablespoons margarine, melted
2 tablespoons brown sugar
½ teaspoon salt
⅛ teaspoon pepper
¼ teaspoon nutmeg
1 egg, beaten
½ cup chopped nuts
1 cup crushed pineapple, drained

sweet potato squash casserole

Combine mashed squash pulp with remaining ingredients. Pour into buttered baking dish. Bake for 30 minutes at 350°F.

Serves 4.

Squash Blossoms

Squash plants bear male and female blossoms. The stem of the female flower eventually begins to swell. This swelling is the squash forming in its initial growth stage. The dried female flower often must be plucked from the end of the mature vegetable. Male blossoms, having long since met their responsibilities in the pollination process, simply fall off and decay. Many gardeners are distressed by this event on the erroneous assumption that these fallen blossoms represent squash which failed to mature.

The male blossoms, easily identified by long, slender stems, can be used by the cook to make several dishes for the table. They may be dipped in thin batter and fried or picked while still in the budding stage and sautéed. Stuffing possibilities are limited only by one's imagination.

1 tablespoon onion, chopped
1½ tablespoons margarine
2 cups cooked spinach or Swiss chard, chopped and drained
1 cup cooked rice
1 egg yolk
½ cup Gruyère, grated
Salt and pepper
8-12 squash blossoms

stuffed squash blossoms

Sauté onion in margarine. Add greens and rice. Mix well. Stir in egg yolk, grated cheese, salt, and pepper. Stuff blossoms and place in buttered baking dish. Heat thoroughly in a moderate oven.

These delicate blossoms also lend themselves very well to a meat stuffing and, as such, may be served as a main dish. Leftover ham, lamb or chicken can be used to make a delicious forcemeat. If you love something spicy, try Italian sausage.

squash blossoms with italian sausage

3 parts ground Italian
   sausage
1 part onion, chopped
1 part green pepper,
   chopped
Tomato sauce
Parmesan cheese
Squash blossoms

Prepare amounts needed using these proportions. Crumble sausage in a skillet and sauté until lightly browned with onion and green pepper. Drain off excess fat. Add enough tomato sauce to bind mixture. Season with Parmesan. Stuff blossoms. Place in greased baking dish and bake in moderate oven until heated through.

For a mouth-watering delicacy, try blossoms stuffed with cream cheese.

blossoms and cream cheese

1 8-ounce package cream
   cheese, softened
1/3 cup onion, minced
Salt and pepper
Chives
Margarine
Capers (optional)
12-14 squash blossoms

Mix cheese, onion and seasonings. Stuff squash blossoms. Sauté gently or place in buttered baking dish. Heat thoroughly in a 300°F. oven.

Zucchini-Vegetable Mixes for Freezing

Many delicious dishes can be prepared easily and quickly from frozen vegetable combinations. These may be served as entities in themselves or combined with meat and other ingredients to become mouth-watering stews, soups, and casseroles.

When the copious bounty of the squash patch starts threatening you, make up several batches of one or more zucchini-vegetable mixes and stack them away in the freezer. Make a list of what you are storing and where, perhaps taping this list to the freezer itself so that anytime you need a vegetable mix, it can be located easily, already partially cooked and ready to pop into a pot or baking dish at a moment's notice.

1 cup onion, minced
1 cup celery, diced
2 tablespoons margarine, melted
2 cups chicken stock or bouillon
2 cups carrots, sliced or diced
2 cups zucchini, sliced or diced
1 cup corn, cut from cob
1 cup green pepper, chopped
Salt and pepper

basic zucchini-vegetable mix

Sauté onion and celery in margarine. Add broth and carrots. Simmer for 20 minutes. Add zucchini, corn, and green pepper and simmer an additional 10 minutes. Season. Pour into freezer container for future use in stews, soups, casseroles, or squash fillings. *Note:* Creamed mixed vegetables are delicious in squash cases.

zucchini-oriental mix

Simmer zucchini, cabbage, and spinach in broth until soft. Add drained sprouts and chestnuts. Season. Freeze. May be heated and served alone or over rice.

2 cups zucchini, sliced or diced
2 cups cabbage, shredded
1 cup fresh spinach, chopped
2 cups chicken stock or bouillon
1 can bean sprouts
1 can water chestnuts
Salt and pepper

1 medium onion, chopped
2 cups zucchini, sliced or diced
2 tablespoons olive oil
1 cup cooked garbanzo beans
2 cups Romano green beans, cut in 2-inch pieces
1 red bell pepper, chopped
2 cups chicken broth or bouillon
Salt and pepper
½ cup green olives, sliced or chopped

zucchini-italiano mix

Sauté onion and zucchini in oil until soft. Add more oil if necessary. Add beans, pepper, and broth. Simmer until vegetables are tender. Season; add olives. Pour into containers and freeze.

another zucchini-vegetable mix

1 cup onion, minced
2 tablespoons olive oil
1 cup celery, chopped
2 cups zucchini, sliced
2 cups chicken stock or bouillon
1 cup peas
1 cup lima beans
1 cups carrots, sliced
  Salt and pepper

Sauté onion and celery in oil. Sauté zucchini in the oil briefly; add stock and remaining vegetables. Simmer for 20 minutes. Season. Cool and pour all ingredients in freezer containers.

zucchini mix in tomato sauce

3 pounds ripe tomatoes, peeled and chopped
¼ cup onion, minced
1 cup celery, chopped
1½-2 pounds zucchini, chopped (5-6 cups)
1 tablespoon sugar or honey
1½ teaspoons salt

Force chopped tomatoes through a food mill or coarse sieve to remove seeds. Sauté onion and celery in oil. Add squash, tomato purée, and sugar. Simmer until reduced and thickened, stirring frequently. Add salt; remove from heat and cool. Ladle into hot sterilized jars or appropriate freezer container leaving ¼ inch headroom for expansion.

zucchini mix in cheese sauce

Sauté onion in margarine. Mix well with flour and gradually add milk, stirring until thick. Add remaining ingredients and cook until cheese is melted. Pour into freezer containers and freeze.

1 medium onion, minced
1/4 cup margarine
1/4 cup flour
2 cups milk
1/2 teaspoon salt
1 tablespoon prepared mustard
1 cup Cheddar cheese, shredded

1 medium zucchini, sliced thinly
1 medium tomato, peeled and chopped
1 medium onion, sliced thinly
Salt and pepper
Margarine

basic zucchini-casserole mix

Sauté seasoned vegetables in margarine until soft. Cool and freeze.

Spaghetti Squash

Spaghetti Squash

Spaghetti squash, a novel cucurbit which is just beginning to fascinate cooks, is frequently described as "vegetable spaghetti."

This squash is easily grown and lends itself very well to some appetizing dishes because it adapts well to most traditional pasta recipes. Its fibrous consistency provides a product which roughly resembles true spaghetti or pasta.

Vegetable spaghetti has one very decided advantage over pasta. It has a very low caloric value and, as such, is a weight watcher's dream. One inveterate dieter, having joyously discovered spaghetti squash at the local farmers' market, left a standing order every week, referring to vegetable spaghetti as a "happening" because she could freely indulge her desires for pasta dishes with gusto and without guilt.

The spaghetti is easily prepared. Boil whole about thirty minutes or bake at 350°F. until the skin begins to give. Baking may take an hour or more, depending upon the size. Halve squash lengthwise and remove the seeds. Fluff up the fibrous content with a fork, until it resembles strands of spaghetti. Spoon sauce or fillings onto spaghetti; return to oven and heat thoroughly. Spaghetti also may be removed from the shell and layered in a casserole, if preferred.

spaghetti squash bake

Make a white sauce by melting margarine in a saucepan, then adding flour and salt. Add milk gradually and stir until thickened. Combine 1 cup of the sauce with spinach and nutmeg. Into a 1-quart casserole pour the remaining sauce. Layer the spinach mixture, spaghetti, cottage cheese, and egg slices. Sprinkle with Parmesan. Bake at 350°F. for 30 minutes.

Serves 2-3.

2 tablespoons margarine
2⅓ tablespoons flour
1 teaspoon salt
1⅓ cups milk
1 cup spinach, cooked, drained and chopped
½ teaspoon nutmeg
1½ cups vegetable spaghetti
½ cup cottage cheese
2 hardboiled eggs, sliced
Parmesan cheese

al burro

Simply toss spaghetti squash with butter (burro), garlic salt and freshly grated Parmesan.

spaghetti squash with chicken livers

Season livers with garlic salt and sauté in oil, but do not brown. Drain and set aside. Add onion and sauté until translucent. Chop livers and combine with onions and wine into baked squash halves. Heat thoroughly in a 350°F. oven.

Serves 4.

½ pound chicken livers
Garlic salt
¼ cup olive oil
1 small onion, minced
½ cup dry white wine
1½ cups spaghetti squash
2 baked spaghetti squash halves

4 slices bacon, cooked and crumbled
1 8-ounce package grated Cheddar cheese
Salt and pepper
1½ cups spaghetti squash

spaghetti squash cheese bake

Combine all ingredients with fluffed-up spaghetti squash. Heat in moderate oven until cheese melts.

Serves 2.

spaghetti squash pie

Mix cooked vegetable spaghetti with tomato sauce, tomato paste, cheese, and cooked beef. Place in pie shell. Beat eggs and pour over squash mixture. Add seasonings. Bake at 350°F. for 25 minutes.

Serves 4.

4 cups vegetable spaghetti, cooked
1 8-ounce can tomato sauce
1 tablespoon tomato paste
½ cup grated Romano cheese
½ pound ground beef
1 9-inch pie crust
2 eggs
    Pinch oregano
    Salt and pepper

Prepare squash as previously described. Serve with one of the following sauces:

½ cup olive oil
1 clove garlic, minced
½ pound ground beef
¼ pound pork sausage
2 cups tomatoes, peeled and chopped
½ cup tomato paste
½ cup beef stock or bouillon
¼ teaspoon oregano
    Salt and pepper

italian

In oil sauté garlic and ground meats until cooked, but not browned. Add remaining ingredients and mix thoroughly. Simmer over low heat for one hour.

2 slices bacon, fried and
   crumbled
1 medium onion, diced
1 clove garlic, minced
1 carrot, minced
⅛ teaspoon thyme
2 cups tomatoes, peeled and
   chopped
2 tablespoons tomato paste
2 cups chicken stock or
   water
½ cup cooked ham, chopped
1 4-ounce can stems and
   pieces of mushrooms
   Salt and pepper

milanese

Fry bacon, drain and set aside. In drippings sauté onion, garlic, and carrot until tender. Add next 4 ingredients and simmer for 1 hour or more until mixture reaches sauce consistency. Add ham and mushrooms to sauce and serve over vegetable spaghetti.

½ cup onion, chopped
1 clove garlic, minced
1 tablespoon margarine,
   melted
1 tablespoon olive oil
3 cups tomatoes, peeled and
   seeded
1 tablespoon tomato paste
¼ teaspoon oregano
2 cups small shrimp, tuna,
   crab, lobster, clams or
   oysters
   Salt and pepper

seafood

Sauté onion and garlic in margarine and oil. Add remaining ingredients, except seafood, and simmer, stirring frequently for 20 minutes. Add seafood, correct seasoning and simmer for 5-7 minutes.

anchovy

Heat butter, olive oil, and oil from anchovies. Add garlic. Reserve 4 anchovy fillets. Chop remainder and add to oil mixture. Add tomatoes, oregano, and parsley. Simmer, stirring frequently for 20 minutes. Serve over vegetable spaghetti with grated cheese and reserved fillets.

¼ cup butter or margarine, melted
¼ cup olive oil
2 tins of anchovy fillets, undrained
1 clove garlic, minced
2 cups tomatoes, peeled, seeded, and drained
¼ teaspoon oregano
2 tablespoons parsley, chopped
Parmesan cheese, grated

3 tablespoons olive oil
1 cup onion, chopped
1 cup celery, diced
1 cup green pepper, chopped
1 small carrot, diced
1 garlic clove, chopped
1½ pounds tomatoes, peeled and chopped
2 tablespoons tomato paste
1 bay leaf
Coarse black pepper, oregano, basil and salt to taste
1 cup zucchini, chopped
Parmesan

vegetables

Place all ingredients except the last two in a covered skillet. Simmer 45 minutes. Add zucchini and cook for 15 minutes more. Spoon over spaghetti squash and sprinkle with Parmesan. *Note:* Sautéed mushrooms may be added just before serving.

Desserts &
Other Sweets

Cake
Candy
Cookies
Custard
Marmalade
Mousse
Parfait
Pie
Pudding

Desserts & Other Sweets

Sugar plums have nothing over squashes when it comes to sweets. Cakes, candies, cookies, custards, marmalades, mousses, parfaits, pies, puddings and tarts may all be made with products of the squash patch.

The pumpkin has been featured as a dessert primarily in pie form for as long as the history of this country has been recorded. However, there are many other ways to use this versatile cucurbit as the following recipes indicate.

Summer squash is usually overlooked when desserts are concocted probably because it is so useful and versatile in other types of dishes. Several zucchini dessert recipes are included, therefore, as an indication that zucchini and other summer cousins should not be ignored when sweets are served.

Cakes

pumpkin cheesecake

Place cream cheese in mixing bowl and beat in sugar until mixture is fluffy. Add beaten eggs gradually. Mix in remaining ingredients. Pour batter into pie crust and place in preheated 325°F. oven. Bake for 80 minutes or until cheesecake is firm around edges. Turn off heat and let cake remain in cooling oven an additional 30 minutes. Cool on rack. May be topped with whipped cream.

4 8-ounce packages cream cheese, softened
1 cup granulated sugar
½ cup brown sugar, packed
5 eggs, beaten
2 cups cooked pumpkin, drained
1 teaspoon cinnamon
½ teaspoon ginger
¼ teaspoon ground cloves
1 teaspoon vanilla
1 9-inch graham cracker crust
Whipped cream for topping

pumpkin cupcakes

Combine all ingredients and mix thoroughly. Fill greased and floured muffin tins ⅔ full. Bake at 350°F. for 15-20 minutes. Place on racks to cool. Serve with butter, honey, or cream cheese.

Makes about 2 dozen 2-inch cakes.

1 cup cooked pumpkin, drained
1 cup biscuit mix
¼ cup cooking oil
½ cup brown sugar, packed
2 eggs, beaten
2 teaspoons baking powder
½ cup milk
½ cup seedless raisins

Cake
2 eggs
1 cup sugar
⅔ cup oil
1¼ cups all-purpose flour
1 teaspoon baking powder
1 teaspoon baking soda
1 teaspoon cinnamon
½ teaspoon salt
1 cup carrot, grated
1 cup zucchini, grated and drained
½ cup chopped nuts
Frosting
1 3-ounce package cream cheese, softened
3 tablespoons margarine
1 teaspoon vanilla
2 cups powdered sugar

zucchini-carrot cake

Cake: Beat eggs with sugar until frothy. Gradually beat in oil. Add dry ingredients. Beat at high speed 4 minutes. Stir in carrot, zucchini, and nuts. Pour into a greased 9-inch square baking pan. Bake in a 350°F. oven about 35 minutes or until top springs back when lightly touched.
Frosting: In small mixer bowl, blend cream cheese and margarine; add sugar and vanilla. Beat until smooth. Spread evenly over cooled cake.

pumpkin-apple torte

Combine pumpkin with eggs and sugar. Stir in flour, baking powder and seasonings. Stir in apples and nuts. Pour batter into greased, floured 8-inch round cake pan. Preheat oven to 325°F. Bake for 20-25 minutes. Test for doneness with toothpick. May be served with whipped topping.

1 cup cooked pumpkin, drained
3 eggs, beaten
1 cup sugar
¾ cup flour
1 teaspoon baking powder
2 teaspoons cinnamon
1 teaspoon ginger
½ teaspoon salt
½ cup apple, pared and chopped
½ cup nuts, chopped
Whipped topping

Candy

2 cups sugar
3 tablespoons pumpkin
¼ teaspoon cornstarch
⅓ teaspoon pumpkin pie spice
½ cup milk, evaporated milk, or cream
½ teaspoon vanilla

pumpkin fudge

Combine the first five ingredients in a saucepan and heat until the mixture passes the "fudge test." This test involves dropping a small amount into cold water and if it forms a ball, the test is passed. Then add the vanilla and beat with mixer until smooth. Pour onto buttered cookie sheet or platter and cut when cool.

Cookies

zucchini bars

Mix melted margarine, oil, and sugar. Beat eggs and combine with water, vanilla, and nutmeg. Add to sugar mixture. Sift flours, salt, and baking soda and add to mixture. Stir in remaining ingredients. Spread into two 7½ × 3½ inch buttered baking pans. Bake at 350°F. for 40 minutes. Cool before cutting.

½ cup margarine, melted
½ cup cooking oil
1½ cups brown sugar, packed
2 eggs
2 tablespoons water
1 teaspoon vanilla
¼ teaspoon nutmeg
1½ cups all-purpose flour
½ cup whole wheat flour
⅓ teaspoon salt
1 teaspoon baking soda
1 cup seedless raisins
1 cup shredded coconut
1½ cups bran cereal buds
2½ cups zucchini, grated and
  drained

3 cups butternut squash,
  peeled and sliced
3 cups tart apples, peeled
  and sliced
1 cup brown sugar, packed
⅛ teaspoon ground cloves
1 teaspoon cinnamon
2 teaspoons lemon juice
1¼ cups all-purpose flour
½ teaspoon salt
6 tablespoons margarine,
  softened
⅓ cup chopped nuts

butternut-apple crisp bars

Mix squash and apple slices with ½ cup brown sugar, cloves, cinnamon, and lemon juice, tossing gently. Place in a shallow casserole and bake at 350°F. for 30 minutes. Combine remaining sugar, flour, salt, and margarine until crumbly; add nuts. Spread evenly in casserole. Bake for 40 minutes longer. Cut into wedges or bars. May be topped with ice cream.

raisin-pumpkin cookies

Sift together flour, salt, soda and spices. Combine vanilla, oil, sugar, egg, and pumpkin pulp and beat well. Add flour mixture and raisins. Mix well. Drip spoonfuls of batter on a buttered cookie sheet, allowing room for expansion. Bake at 350°F. for 20 minutes or until cookies are browned.

Makes 4 dozen.

2½ cups all-purpose flour
½ teaspoon salt
½ teaspoon baking soda
¼ teaspoon cinnamon
½ teaspoon nutmeg
¼ teaspoon ginger
½ teaspoon vanilla
¾ cup cooking oil
1¼ cups brown sugar
1 egg
1 cup cooked pumpkin, mashed
2 cups seedless raisins

Custard

1 cup sugar
2 eggs, beaten
1 cup cooked pumpkin pulp
½ cup brown sugar
½ teaspoon cinnamon
¼ teaspoon ginger
1 cup milk

caramelized pumpkin custard

Make caramel by heating and stirring sugar over medium heat until melted. Pour into greased loaf pan. Beat eggs with remaining ingredients, blending thoroughly. Pour mixture over caramelized sugar. Place custard pan in larger pan of hot water. Bake at 350°F. until custard is set. Test with knife. Custard will need to bake about 1 hour. Chill. To serve, loosen edge of custard with knife. Place a lid over custard pan and invert quickly. Individual custard cups may be used if preferred, and it may be made without caramel. Cooked winter squash may be added to any custard; just decrease milk ½ cup for each cup of squash.

Marmalade

zucchini marmalade

Peel squash and slice. Place in kettle with lemon juice, peel and pineapple. Bring to boil. Lower heat and simmer uncovered for 15 minutes. Add pectin and bring to boil. Stir in sugar and ginger at full rolling boil 1 minute, stirring constantly. Remove from heat; skim off foam. Allow mixture to cool for 5 minutes. Skim and ladle into hot sterilized jars and seal with paraffin.

Makes 5 pints.

2 pounds young summer squash
Juice of 2 lemons
1 teaspoon grated lemon peel
1 can (13½ ounces) crushed pineapple, drained
1 package powdered pectin
5 cups sugar
2 tablespoons chopped crystallized ginger

zucchini conserve

5 pounds zucchini
4½ cups sugar
⅓ cup peach or apricot brandy
¼ cup water
½ cup seedless raisins, chopped
¼ cup pecans, chopped
Dark rum

Cut squash into very thin slices. Combine sugar, brandy, and water. Stir over low heat until sugar dissolves. Add zucchini and simmer until squash becomes transparent. Add raisins and nuts and mix well. With slotted spoon, fill pint sterilized jars with conserve to within ½ inch of rim. Add one tablespoon dark rum to each jar and fill to within ¼ inch of top with the remaining syrup boiling hot. Seal jars according to manufacturer's directions.

Makes 2 pints.

Mousse

pumpkin mousse

Sprinkle gelatin over brandy in top of double boiler. Add sugars and spices until gelatin is dissolved. Add pumpkin pulp and milk. Mix thoroughly and chill until mixture thickens. Beat whipping cream until peaks form. Fold into pumpkin mixture. Pour into lightly greased 4-cup mold.

2 envelopes unflavored gelatin
½ cup brandy
½ cup brown sugar
½ cup granulated sugar
1 teaspoon cinnamon
1 teaspoon nutmeg
½ teaspoon ground cloves
½ teaspoon salt
2 cups cooked pumpkin pulp
1 cup milk
2 cups whipping cream

Parfait

1 package vanilla pudding mix
¼ cup light brown sugar
½ teaspoon cinnamon
¼ teaspoon ginger
1½ cups milk
1 cup pumpkin, cooked and mashed

pumpkin parfait

Combine dry ingredients. Heat milk to boiling. Add pumpkin and dry ingredients. Mix well. Spoon into serving glasses. Top with whipped cream, if desired.

Pies

winter squash pie

Combine squash, milk, eggs, rum, and vanilla. Mix thoroughly. Stir in all other ingredients. Pour batter into pie shell. Bake in preheated 300°F. oven for 1 hour.

1½ cups cooked squash or pumpkin
1 cup evaporated milk
3 eggs, beaten
¼ cup rum
½ teaspoon vanilla
¾ cup sugar
4 tablespoons brown sugar
1 teaspoon cinnamon
½ teaspoon ginger
¼ teaspoon ground ginger
½ teaspoon salt
10-inch pie shell, baked

1 package unflavored gelatin
¼ cup water
2 cups sugar
¼ cup peach or apricot brandy
2 cups zucchini, sliced thinly
½ cup seedless raisins, chopped
2 peaches, fresh or canned, sliced
2 tablespoons brown sugar
9-inch pie crust, baked

zucchini-raisin pie

Dissolve gelatin in water. In a saucepan combine with sugar and brandy; heat until sugar dissolves. Add zucchini slices and simmer until squash becomes transparent. Add raisins and mix well. Pour into baked pie shell. Layer with peach slices and drizzle with sugar. Place in a 350°F. oven until brown sugar melts. Garnish with whipped cream, if desired.

butternut custard pie

Beat all ingredients together in large bowl. Pour into 9-inch pie shell. Pour any leftover filling into custard cups. Bake at 400°F. for 10 minutes, then at 350°F. for 50 minutes until custard is set.

2 eggs, beaten
½ teaspoon cinnamon
½ teaspoon allspice
¼ teaspoon ground cloves
¾ cup brown sugar, tightly packed
1¼ cup rich milk
¼ cup dark corn syrup
1 teaspoon salt
2 cups butternut, cooked and mashed
9-inch pie shell, baked

1 9-inch graham cracker crust
1 envelope unflavored gelatin
¾ cup brown sugar
½ teaspoon salt
½ teaspoon ginger
¼ teaspoon nutmeg
1 teaspoon cinnamon
½ cup milk
2 cups pumpkin, cooked and mashed
2 egg yolks, beaten
1 teaspoon vanilla
2 egg whites, stiffly beaten
½ cup whipping cream
⅓ cup granulated sugar

pumpkin chiffon pie

Prepare graham cracker crust. Combine gelatin, brown sugar, seasonings, milk, pumpkin, and egg yolks. Bring to a boil while stirring. Allow to cool; add vanilla. Fold in egg whites. Whip cream, gradually adding sugar, until stiff. Fold into pumpkin mixture. Pour into crust and chill until firm. Garnish with additional whipped cream, if desired.

pumpkin ice cream pie

1½ cups pumpkin pulp,
    mashed and drained
½ cup brown sugar
¼ teaspoon salt
½ teaspoon cinnamon
¼ teaspoon nutmeg
¼ teaspoon ginger
1 quart vanilla ice cream,
    softened
1 9-inch graham cracker
    crust
¼ cup toasted nuts, chopped
    Whipped topping

Combine first 6 ingredients. Fold into ice cream. Spoon into prepared pie shell. Sprinkle with chopped nuts. May be garnished with whipped topping.

1½ cups pumpkin pulp,
    cooked and mashed
1½ cups milk
1 3-ounce package vanilla
    pudding mix
⅓ cup brown sugar
½ teaspoon cinnamon
½ teaspoon ginger
8 4-inch individual tart shells,
    baked
Topping
  ⅓ cup orange marmalade
  ¼ cup brown sugar
  1 cup chopped nuts

pumpkin-nut tarts

Combine ingredients in a saucepan and bring to a boil, stirring constantly. Pour into prepared tart shells and chill.
Topping: Combine ⅓ cup orange marmalade and ¼ cup brown sugar in a saucepan. Heat, while stirring, until sugar dissolves. Simmer 3 minutes. Add 1 cup chopped nuts. Spoon on tart, still warm, at serving time.

Puddings

steamed pumpkin pudding

Lightly grease individual ramekins or 1 6½-cup mold. Combine all ingredients and beat thoroughly with electric mixer. Pour mixture into ramekins until ½ full. Cover with foil and tie securely. Place ramekins on rack in kettle with ½ inch water. Cover and steam until pudding sets. Serve with a hot lemon or orange sauce.

1 cup pumpkin or squash
  pulp, cooked and mashed
1½ cups sifted all-purpose
  flour
½ cup granulated sugar
½ cup brown sugar
1 teaspoon baking soda
2 tablespoons orange juice
¾ teaspoon cinnamon
½ teaspoon ground cloves
¼ teaspoon ground ginger
½ teaspoon nutmeg
¼ cup seedless raisins
⅓ cup margarine
1 egg
¼ cup milk

2 pounds pumpkin, cooked
  and mashed
1 tablespoon salt
3 eggs
2 tablespoons margarine
½ teaspoon cinnamon
½ teaspoon nutmeg
⅓ cup flour
⅓ cup sugar
⅓ cup cream

puerto rican pumpkin pudding

Fold pumpkin into combined remaining ingredients. Pour mixture into buttered baking dish or individual ramekins. Bake in a 400°F. oven for 45 minutes.

The Squash Harvest

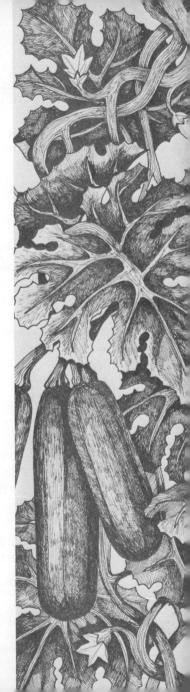

Canning
Freezing
Cooking Frozen Food
Drying
Storing

The Squash Harvest

Canning

Since a boiling water bath is only suitable for high acid fruits and vegetables namely tomatoes (which actually are a fruit), we cannot use this basic canning method for either winter or summer squash.

Naturally squash pickles are the exception because of the vinegar (high acid) content. So unless you already have a pressure cooker or intend to acquire one which may be used for processing canned vegetables, your squash crop belongs in the freezer with all other low acid produce. You may wish to dry some when the freezer is full.

Summer Squash. Zucchini, cocozelle, crookneck, and all other summer varieties may be pressure canned using either a raw pack or hot pack method. In either case, the squash should be carefully washed and sliced.

Raw Pack: Sterilize pint or quart jars. Pack squash tightly. Pour in boiling water to within ½ inch of jar top, making sure all squash is covered. Add salt, ½ teaspoon per pint, and fasten lids firmly. Process at 10 pounds pressure for 25 minutes for pints jars, 30 minutes for quarts.

Hot Pack: Wash and slice squash. Cover with water to which salt has been added. Bring to a rolling boil and remove from heat. Drain and reserve liquid. Pack squash in hot sterilized jars, filling to within ½ inch of top with reserved cooking liquid. Seal and process at 10 pounds pressure for 30 minutes for pints, 40 minutes for quarts.

Winter Squash and Pumpkins. Winter squash and pumpkins may be cubed or mashed for canning. Since most recipes call for mashed pulp, it seems logical to can it in this state. However, if time is short at processing time and there is no shortage of jars, cubing the vegetable is a shorter process and, therefore, may be preferable. Both types of preparation are adaptable to hot pack canning.

Cubed: Cut squash or pumpkin into one-inch cubes after removing seeds and stringy portion. Pare. Place in large pot or kettle, adding boiling water to cover. Allow liquid to resume a rolling boil. Drain vegetable, reserving liquid. Fill hot sterilized jars with hot vegetable, fill to within ½ inch with hot reserved liquid. Add ½ teaspoon salt per pint. Seal and process in pressure cooker at 10 pounds pressure for 60 minutes per pint, 80 minutes per quart.

Mashed: Cut vegetable into several pieces.

Remove seeds and stringy portion. Steam, boil or bake at 350°F. until pulp is soft. Remove skin and mash. Stir over very low heat until thoroughly heated. Pack to within ½ inch of jar top. Seal and process at 10 pounds pressure for 60 minutes per pint or 80 minutes per quart.

Storage of Canned Goods. What a beautiful and satisfying sight — shelf after shelf lined with colorful jars of home-canned produce! Cucurbits, in their many varieties and diverse forms, can make many contributions to a stored supply of delicious and nutritious vegetables. Stews, casseroles, soups, and lots of other dishes created from the canned ingredients-in-waiting, will please many a hungry soul in the months to come.

Assuming care and precision have been the watchwords of the canning process, that only suitable and perfect equipment (especially jars and lids) has been used, then only proper storage conditions are needed to make the products of your own canning factory a total economic and gastronomic success.

Freezing

All squash, both summer and winter, must be blanched prior to freezing. This involves heating the vegetable in either boiling water or steam for a sufficient amount of time to stop enzyme action or the ripening process. To blanch, place sliced or cubed squash in a wire basket or sieve and lower into boiling water. As soon as the water reaches a rolling boil, covering all of the squash, begin timing. When the time is up, lift basket from water, allowing it to drain and immediately put blanched squash into a large bowl of ice water. Fill basket with more squash while waiting for blanching water to return to a boil. Submerge basket and begin process all over again. Squash should remain in cold water bath for the same amount of time that it was submerged in boiling water. Once a blanching-cooling-draining-packing routine is established on a production line basis, you quickly become very efficient in preparing produce for the freezer.

When the squash has cooled, drain it well and pack into a suitable container, label and stack your winter supply of beautiful vegetables in your freezer. Squash keeps well, although most authorities suggest that everything within a freezer, regardless of keeping qualities, should have at least an annual turnover.

Summer Squash. Slice and blanch all summer squash for 3 minutes. A cooling period of 3 minutes also is required. Pack in freezer container leaving at least ½ inch headroom to allow for expansion. Seal and freeze.

Winter Squash. Winter squash adapts well to winter storage in the cellar or in a garage that has protection from freezing temperatures. For this reason, few people devote any precious freezer se vegetables. If space is no issue, however, ...ter squash may be cubed or sliced and blanched, cooled and packed. If preferred, ..ter squash and pumpkin may be precooked until tender, mashed, and the pulp frozen. In either case, cut pumpkin or squash into manageable pieces. Scoop out seeds and stringy portions. Cook until blanched or steam until flesh is soft. Remove skin, mash pulp, cool and pack. *Note:* Spaghetti squash may be frozen whole. Simply blanch in boiling water for 10-12 minutes. Immerse in ice water the same length of time. Then slip it into a plastic bag or wrap in foil and place in the freezer. To thaw, expose squash to room temperature 50-60 minutes. Boil whole for 30-45 minutes depending upon size.

Freezer Containers. Containers of various sizes and descriptions are available commercially. Square containers waste the least amount of space in freezers. Wide mouth canning jars also accommodate frozen produce; the wide opening is designed to facilitate the removal of still frozen food. Freezer bags are also available, including the heat-seal variety in which the food may be cooked in boiling water. An at-home sealing mechanism is commercially available.

Frugality often promotes the use of recycled dairy containers such as those for quarts and 1/2 gallons of milk, 8 and 16 ounces of cottage cheese, yogurt, etc. Recycled coffee cans, used alone or lined with plastic bags and sealed with their own plastic lids, make useful freezer containers, holding approximately 3 1/2 cups of frozen food per 1-pound can.

All packages should be air-tight. Freezer bags must be squeezed to expel all air. The bag tops should be twisted, doubled back and fastened securely with wire or rubber bands. Recycled dairy and coffee containers should be taped at the opening with freezer or masking tape which then can be labeled with an indelible pen.

Cooking Frozen Food

Most cooks overextend their cooking enthusiasm and cook vegetables too long. This reduces nutritional value, and flavor, texture, and appearance are also victims of overcooking.

Frozen squash is best prepared without gradual thawing. For every pint of frozen squash, heat 1/2 cup of salted water to a rolling boil. Add squash; allow boiling to resume. Reduce heat and gently simmer for 10 minutes. If squash has been frozen in cooking bags, simply immerse bag into boiling water, reduce heat and simmer as above, allowing 3-5 minutes of additional cooking time.

Drying

One of the oldest methods of preserving garden, orchard and berry patch produce is drying. If you are weary of canning or have run out of jars and the freezer is bulging, why not dry some of the surplus squash?

The drying process is a time-consuming one, too much so for some of its detractors. There is only one way to discover whether drying has any merits from your perspective and that is to try it, at least on a small scale, and make your own decision whether to try this preserving method again.

Squash is one of several vegetables which adapt to the drying process. Onions, peppers, carrots, and beans also may be preserved in this manner. So too can many fruits, such as plums, apples, grapes, and apricots, which are expensive when bought at the supermarket.

Perhaps an experiment in drying surplus zucchini will convince you of certain economical advantages which you may apply later to other home-grown produce.

Dryers are available commercially. New varieties are being introduced continually. Articles on the drying process appear with increasing frequency in all gardening periodicals. These occurrences indicate an ever-widening interest in drying fruits and vegetables at home.

In primitive times, drying was accomplished by using the only dryer available — the sun. Solar drying is possible today in geographical areas where the heat is intense enough, the air is dry enough and the individuals involved have sufficient patience. A bed sheet spread out in a sunny spot is all that is needed for equipment. If it can be spread over an old window screen and suspended or supported enough to allow for bottom air circulation, so much the better. The racked, drying vegetables must be brought inside at sunset since nighttime moisture would defeat your purpose. More elaborate drying systems call for the use of specially constructed trays, designed to fit your oven, or independent drying boxes either of the homemade or purchased variety. Directions for construction and use of such equipment can be obtained by writing to the Office of Information, U.S. Department of Agriculture, Washington, D.C., 20250, requesting Bulletin 984, Farm and Home Drying of Fruits and Vegetables.

Squash does not lend itself to drying as easily as other garden produce, and certain precautions must be taken. Pumpkin was preserved in pioneer homes simply by cutting it into chunks and stringing it to hang with other vegetables, fruits and even meats to dry over the wood stove. Today we slice both squash and pumpkin and steam blanch for 6-8 minutes. Some prefer to shred these vegetables for faster drying, and dried squash adapts best to recipes in which it is mashed.

Squash and pumpkin may be dried on racks in an oven set at 140°F. The oven door should be left ajar to allow for some air circulation. Cheesecloth spread over oven racks may suffice although more suitable equipment is easily constructed.

The drying process is a lengthy one; an infinite supply of patience is recommended. When the vegetables finally become brittle, they should be removed from the oven or dryer and conditioned for several days. In a large non-metal crock or jar

tainer, allow dried material to condition
ventilated room for a week or more. Stir
oles each day. Cover container with netting
cheesecloth to avoid attracting insects. As a final
precaution against spoilage, oven pasteurization is
highly recommended. Spread dried squash or
pumpkin on racks again; preheat to 175°F. and give
vegetables a 10-minute exposure to this heat. Cool
completely; pack in glass jars; seal and store in a
cool dry place.

Storing Squash

Zucchini, cocozelle, crookneck and all other
related summer squash must be canned, frozen or
dried as they cannot be winter-stored successfully.

Winter squash and all other tough-skinned varieties keep well when stored properly in cool, dry
areas such as basements, root cellars, attics and
some minimally heated garages. The ideal temperature is between 45° and 60°F. Pumpkins, including the cushaw, prefer somewhat cooler surround-
ings from 35° to 40°F. No cucurbit can survive
extended exposure to below-freezing temperatures.

All squash and pumpkins should be handled
gently for they bruise and dent easily. Such wounds
encourage spoilage in even the healthiest of
specimens.

For maximum storage condition, cut squash and
pumpkin from the vine, retaining a stem of at least
one inch in length. It is tempting, when caught in
the garden without a knife, to simply tug away at a
squash, wrenching it stemless from the umbilical
vine. Use a sharp knife. Allow your storage crop to
cure outdoors in a sunny spot for about two weeks.
Cured in this manner, your cucurbits may be packed
off to the storage area to be placed on shelves in
single layers and not touching, or wrapped individ-
ually in newspaper and stacked in crates or baskets.
They then will last most of the winter.